NEW INDIAN SKETCHES

Reverend Pierre-Jean De Smet, Pioneer Jesuit Missionary of the Northwest
Original in the Jesuit Provincial Archives at Gonzaga University.

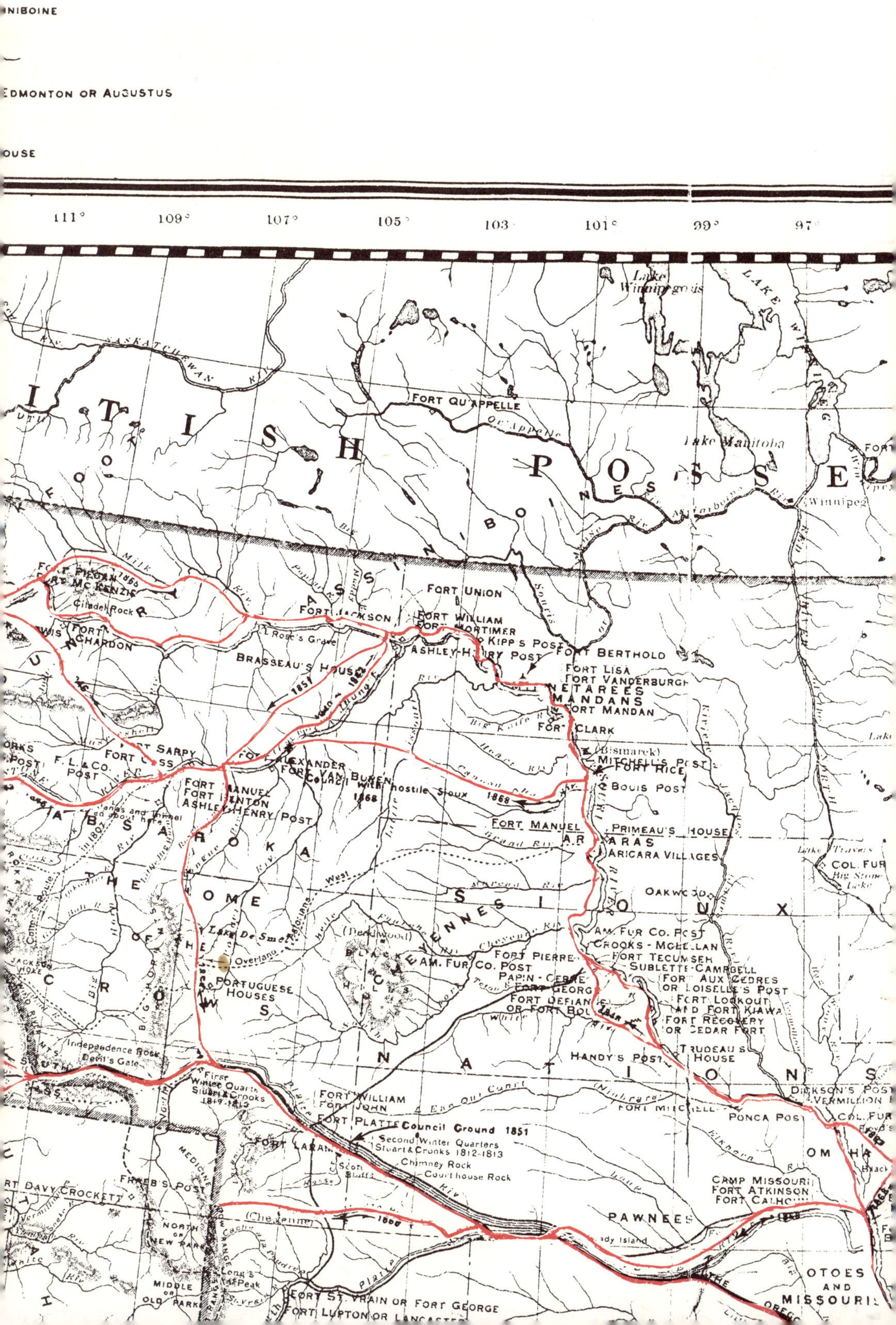
INIBOINE
EDMONTON OR AUGUSTUS
OUSE
111°
109°
107°
105°
103°
101°
99°
97°
Lake Winnipegosis
LAKE WINNIPEG
SASKATCHEWAN RIV.
FORT QU'APPELLE
Qu'Appelle
Lake Manitoba
Winnipeg
BRITISH POSSESSIONS
ASSINIBOINES
FORT PIEGAN 1856
FORT MC KENZIE
Citadel Rock
FORT CHARDON
Rose's Grave
FORT JACKSON
FORT UNION
FORT WILLIAM
FORT MORTIMER
KIPP'S POST
ASHLEY-HENRY POST
FORT BERTHOLD
BRASSEAU'S HOUSE
FORT LISA
FORT VANDERBURGH
MINNETAREES
MANDANS
FORT MANDAN
FORT CLARK
Big Knife R.
(Bismarck)
MITCHELL'S POST
FORT RICE
FORT SARPY
FORT CASS
F. L. & CO. POST
FORT ALEXANDER
FORT VAN BUREN
Council with hostile Sioux 1868
1868
BOUIS POST
FORT MANUEL
FORT BENTON
ASHLEY-HENRY POST
FORT MANUEL
PRIMEAU'S HOUSE
ABSAROKA
ARICARA VILLAGES
Grand Riv.
Moreau Riv.
OAKWOOD
SIOUX
Lake Traverse
COL. FUR
Big Stone Lake
HOME OF THE CROWS
Lake De Smet
(Deadwood)
CHEYENNES
Cheyenne Riv.
AM. FUR CO. POST
CROOKS - MCCLELLAN
FORT TECUMSEH
SUBLETTE-CAMPBELL
FORT PIERRE
AM. FUR CO. POST
PAPIN - CERRE
FORT GEORGE
FORT DEFIANCE OR FORT BOULIS
FORT AUX CEDRES OR LOISELLE'S POST
FORT LOOKOUT AND FORT KIAWA
FORT RECOVERY OR CEDAR FORT
Overland
PORTUGUESE HOUSES
BLACK HILLS
Independence Rock
Devil's Gate
NATIONS
HANDY'S POST
TRUDEAU'S HOUSE
DICKSON'S POST
VERMILLION
First Winter Quarters Stuart & Crooks 1811-1812
FORT WILLIAM
FORT JOHN
FORT PLATTE
Council Ground 1851
FORT LARAMIE
Second Winter Quarters Stuart & Crooks 1812-1813
Scott's Bluffs
Chimney Rock
Court house Rock
FORT MITCHELL
PONCA POST
COL. FUR
OMAHA
Elkhorn
FRAEB'S POST
FORT DAVY CROCKETT
NORTH OR NEW PARK
MEDICINE BOW RANGE
CAMP MISSOURI
FORT ATKINSON
FORT CALHOUN
(Cheyenne)
PAWNEES
Grand Island
MIDDLE OR OLD PARK
Long's Peak
FORT ST. VRAIN OR FORT GEORGE
FORT LUPTON OR LANCASTER
OTOES AND MISSOURIS
Platte Riv.

NEW INDIAN SKETCHES

REV. P.J. DE SMET, S.J.

INTRODUCTION AND EDITING BY
EDWARD J. KOWRACH

YE GALLEON PRESS
FAIRFIELD, WASHINGTON

It is a good thing to give thanks . . . .

The photograph of Reverend Pierre-Jean De Smet printed facing the title page is from the Jesuit Provincial Archives, Gonzaga University.

I wish to thank Lawrence Aripa for permission to use his drawing of the Sacred Heart mission and Louise Sighouin that we printed on page 24.

Ye Galleon Press
Fairfield, Washington 99012

Of this edition ___________ copies were printed.

This is Copy Number ___________.

Library of Congress Cataloging in Publication Data

Smet, Pierre-Jean de, 1801-1873.
New Indian sketches.

Bibliography: p.
Includes index.
1.Indians of North America—West (U.S.)—Missions. 2. Skitswish Indians—Missions. 3. Smet, Pierre-Jean de, —West (U.S.) I. Kowrach, Edward J. II. Title.

E78.W5S58 1985 266'.2796 84-27021
ISBN 0-87770-335-3

TABLE OF CONTENTS

NEW INDIAN SKETCHES

INTRODUCTION

Considering the difficulties and the primitive modes of travel in the western United States in the early nineteenth century, it is hardly believeable to read of the amount of travel that Father Pierre-Jean De Smet recorded from his home base at St. Louis. His first extended trip west in 1840 to the Flathead Indians was along the Oregon Trail by wagon train. In 1841 he again came the same way and from that time on all his traveling west was by boat on the rivers or by horseback or on foot, until his first journey by rail to Cheyenne, Wyoming in 1868. His travels were mostly for the purpose of collecting funds for the Rocky Mountain Mission and to find priests, Brothers, and Sisters to staff these missions.

The principal aim of this introduction is to specifically detail the travels of Father De Smet in the Pacific Northwest in relation to present-day locations and state boundaries so that a reader can more easily trace the missionary's travels

The contacts and travels among the various Plateau Indians of the Northwest mentioned in the records are extensive. He met with the various tribes of Assiniboines, Blackfeet, Chaudiere, Chewelah, Coeur d'Alene, Colville, Cree, Crow, Flatbow, Flatheads, Kalispell, Kootenay, Gens de Lac, Nez Perce, Okanogan, Pend d'Oreille, Snakes, Shoshone, Simpoil, Spokane, and the Yakima. Most of these Indians were well-disposed and greeted De Smet cordially. As with all classes of men some few radicals were warriors and trouble-makers whom he could not reach.

The beginning of Father De Smet's long association with the northwest Indians was a direct result of his meeting in 1839 with the last of the four Indian deputations to St. Louis. This deputation of two Indians, Peter Gaucher and Young Ignace was successful. In descending the Missouri River they stopped at Council Bluffs at St. Joseph Mission. There they met Father De Smet who was to answer their plea. He later wrote: "On the 18th of last September (1835) two Catholic Iroquois came to visit us. They had been for twenty-three years among the nation called Flatheads and Pierced Noses . . . I have never seen any savages so fervent in religion. By their instructions and examples they have given all that nation a great desire to have themselves baptized . . . The sole object of these good Iroquois was to obtain a priest to come and finish what they had so happily commenced . . . We gave them letters of recommendation." The two Indians finally arrived at St. Louis and when they presented themselves to Bishop Joseph Rosati, C.M. with De Smet's letters they were given definite promises of a priest for next spring. With this news Gaucher set out immediately to return to the Flathead Indians and Young Ignace remained to lead the Black Robe back next spring.

Father De Smet volunteered to go as their missionary. At first it was decided to send two priests but because of the shortage of funds Father De Smet was permitted to go alone. He was to survey the needs and report back to his superiors.

FIRST JOURNEY WEST

On the 27th of March 1840 De Smet set out from St. Louis. By steamboat he went to Westport and then he joined the annual expedition of the American Fur Company to the mountains. They traveled the Oregon Trail to the Rendezvous on the Green River. Here he met a deputation of ten Flathead Indians sent to meet him. After four days at the Rendezvous they left going north through Jackson Hole and across the Teton Pass into Pierre's Hole. Here was the temporary camp of about 1600 Flatheads and Pend d'Oreilles who had come to welcome the longed-for Black Robe. They greeted him with sincere demonstrations of joy. The Father at once began a series of instructions. All the Indians present eagerly started to learn their prayers and moral obligations to the Great Spirit.

After a short stay at Pierre's Hole the whole entourage moved slowly along the Henry Fork of the Snake River to its source at Henry Lake where they arrived on the 22nd of July. They stayed here a week and then in the next month Father De Smet and the Flatheads trouped at an easy pace across the Continental Divide to Red Rock Lake following the river that leads to the Jefferson River to the Three Forks of the Missouri. For about a month, the priest spent much time instructing the Indians and sizing up the prospects of further missionary work among them. He felt that these natives showed genuine promise for conversion. He did not actually get into the Flathead country which lay west of the Continental Divide in present western Montana along the Bitterroot River.

As time was running short, Father De Smet promised the Flatheads that he would hasten to report to his superiors and get the necessary funds and personnel to establish a permanent mission next spring in their midst. Seventeen natives, as an escort, led De Smet to the Yellowstone River and from thence with a Flemish trapper-friend, De Velder, he descended the Missouri to St. Louis where he arrived December 31st. The glowing report of promised success among the Indians was made to the Bishop and his Jesuit superiors. However, the critical problem of funding arose. De Smet contacted Bishop Francis P. Kenrick of Philadelphia for financial help which he received. He also went to New Orleans and returned with over $1000 in cash plus other useful articles.

SECOND JOURNEY TO THE FLATHEADS

Divine Providence blessed the project of Father De Smet and on April 24th he left St. Louis. With him from Westport on the Oregon Trail, were Father Nicholas Point, forty-two, a native of France: Father Gregory Mengarini, twenty-nine, an Italian; Jesuit Brothers William Claessens, a Belgian, twenty-nine, a blacksmith; Charles Huet, a Belgian, thirty-five, a carpenter; and Joseph Specht, a German, thirty-two, a tinner. On May 10th they left Westport arriving at Fort Hall, in present-day Idaho, August 14th where they met some waiting Flatheads. The missionaries again crossed the Continental Divide to the Beaver Head River, in western Montana, near where they met the main body of the Flathead nation, led by Little Chief Insula, later baptized Michael. The happy group again crossed the Rockies and followed Deer Creek and Hell-Gate River to the Bitterroot Valley, near present-day Stevensville. They established here St. Mary's Mission, on the right bank of the Bitterroot River on September 24, 1841.

The Bitterroot Valley where the mission was placed was exceedingly fertile, well-watered by streams and enclosed by lofty snow-capped mountains. Thus protected by the mountains the winters were mild. Wild animal life was abundant and the streams abounded in trout. The Lewis and Clark expedition had come through the valley in 1805 going west.

TRIP TO FORT COLVILE (cf. Appendix A)

Though the priests had brought many necessities with them from St. Louis, when they began laying out the new mission, it was seen that they needed more provisions, tools and seeds for the next season. Father De Smet then proceeded to the Hudson's Bay post of Fort Colvile on the Columbia River. Ten Flathead Indians accompanied him as guides. Father De Smet met no hostiles on the trail up the Bitter Root Valley to the Clark Fork River. Down it they went to Pend d'Oreille Lake, then down the Pend d'Oreille River to the present site of Cusick, Washington, where they met the Kalispells for the first time. There the travelers changed their mode of travel to horses and followed the "Flowery Trail" west to the Colville Valley. Thence up to Fort Colvile where they arrived November 14th.

Archibald McDonald, the Chief Factor at the post, received Father De Smet cordially and supplied those tools, plows and seeds needed at the mission. In the four days here the priest met the "eight to nine hundred" Indians of the neighborhood. While giving them brief instructions, baptizing the children and the sick and dying, he saw their sincerity and eagerness and he promised to send them a Black Robe in the future. (In 1845 the first permanent mission was established here.) Kettle Falls then was one of the much frequented salmon fishing spots on the Columbia. Many Indians of the surrounding interior gathered here during the salmon runs. One native reported an estimate of up to 6000 Indians assembled in one fishing season.

Returning by the same route, the group was now laden down with provisions. Father De Smet met the Kalispels again, this time on Horse Prairie, and spent three days with them. The caravan arrived at St. Mary's Mission on the Bitterroot River December 8th. Christmas holidays and spring were spent here, daily instructing the natives and preparing the Mission for the spring planting.

TO FORT VANCOUVER

In the spring of 1842, Father De Smet left with two Canadians and two Indian companions for Fort Vancouver. He wrote, he was not "able this year to obtain either provisions or sufficient clothes to supply the wants of the mission." Also, he wished to meet the only other Catholic missionaries then in the Northwest, Fathers F.N. Blanchet and Modeste Demers, who, in 1838, had come to the Oregon Territory from Quebec, Canada.

The De Smet group, leaving St. Mary's Mission, were met by a band of Coeur d'Alenes who insisted keenly that the priest visit their tribe. He followed them to the shores of Coeur d'Alene Lake where again the Indians urged fervently that a Black Robe be sent them. The Coeur d'Alenes to this day tell of the first three day visit of Father De Smet to their country. (The following fall Father Nicolas Point and Brother C. Huet were sent to the Coeur d'Alene nation.) The De Smet entourage then went down the Spokane Valley, met the Spokane Indians and thence went up to Fort Colvile. The Hudson's Bay Company express was delayed leaving, so Father De Smet made a hundred mile trip up to the main village of the Okanogan Indians. As he moved about this country he was accompanied by hundreds of mounted Indians. The Company express started down the Columbia on May 30th. De Smet writes: "Mr. Ogden [Peter Skene] one of the principal proprietors offered me a place in his [barge]. . . I shall never forget the kindness and friendly manner with which this gentleman treated me throughout the journey". Two barges departed and at The Dalles one was caught in a whirlpool. (only three men in that barge were saved from drowning.) Fortunately Father De Smet had got out to walk along the shore. The party stopped at Fort Okanogan and Fort Walla Walla. Fort Vancouver was reached on the 8th of June.

Here Father De Smet met Dr. John McLoughlin for the first time. This worthy gentleman gave "me every possible proof of interest." De Smet also met Fathers F.N. Blanchet and Modeste Demers. The urgent needs of the missionaries for personnel to assist them were discussed and plans formulated.

It was at this juncture that De Smet for the first time learned of Father F.N. Blanchet's teaching device termed the *Catholic Ladder.* The first two missionaries had with noticeable success used it with the various Indian tribes. De Smet later developed this *Ladder* and published a more sophisticated version. He was enthusiastic about it and said that "this *Ladder* should be used in teaching throughout the world".

In a large Hudson's Bay Company canoe Father De Smet left for the interior. Father Demers accompanied him to Fort Walla Walla. At this point De Smet and an interpreter left to continue the journey to St. Mary's Mission on horseback. On the road they met some Nez Perces and Spokane Indians who generously offered some salmon. After again visiting the Coeur d'Alenes the travelers arrived July 27th at the Mission. In his report Father De Smet summarized the missionary efforts of himself, Fathers Mengarini and Point; together they had baptized to that date 1,654 Indians and Whites.

Sunday July 31 De Smet left St. Mary's Mission with an escort of six Flathead guides and warriors. He visited a large Crow village on the Madison River and continued on the Missouri River on to St. Louis where he arrived three months later October 30th. During this year he had traveled from St. Louis to the Pacific Coast and back, a distance of about five thousand miles safely protected by Divine Providence.

ON TO EUROPE

Before leaving for Europe Father De Smet escorted Fathers Peter DeVos, a Belgian and Adrian Hoecken of Holland and Brother Michael McGean to Westport. He sent them on to the Rocky Mountain Missions and he turned about to go to New York to board ship June 7, 1843 for Europe to solicit funds and personnel. After twenty-one days sailing, he landed in Ireland.

From whence he toured the capitals of Europe visiting numerous convents and monasteries. His efforts were extremely successful. He sailed from Antwerp, Belgium, January 9, 1844 to return to Oregon Territory on the ship *L'Indefatigable,* under Captain Moller, around the Horn of South America. He brought along a priest and Brother from Belgium, three Italian priests and six Sisters of Notre Dame de Namur, "with about 80 tons of sundries. . . a few things, such as fire arms and tobacco, being adapted for the Indian trade." The ship crossed the dangerous Columbia River bar safely July 31st after nearly seven months of sailing. De Smet with some Indians in a dugout canoe preceded the party to Fort Vancouver. Five days later the slow ship arrived at the fort. All were greated by Dr. McLoughlin, the staff and Indians of the post, as the first *Lady Black Robes* stepped ashore. Nine days later the group set out for St. Paul Mission on the Willamette River.

On the banks of the river at St. Paul, a site was chosen for the Jesuit "Motherhouse", titled St. Francis Xavier. This was to be the central Jesuit administration headquarters. The Sisters of Notre Dame began organizing a school for Whites and Indians nearby, under the direction of Father Blanchet.

WITH THE KALISPELLS

After the Willamette headquarters were established Father De Smet embarked for the interior on October 3rd. Elkanah Walker, the Protestant missionary to the Spokanes wrote in his diary, "that they went through the Tshimakain Mission Sat. Nov. 2."

On November 6th De Smet met Father Adrian Hoecken on the Pend d'Oreille River where a site was chosen for a new mission among the Kalispels. In 1841 De Smet met them on his first trip to Fort Colvile. These natives had learned their prayers from the Flatheads previously and earnestly indicated they longed for a missionary. Because winter came on early Father De Smet was forced to stay over Christmas here lodged in a small hut "well-chosen, picturesque, agreeable and convenient . . . with abundant fuel . . . encircled by ranges of lofty mountains . . . with thousands of deer." The Midnight Mass was celebrated with "general firing of guns . . . and 300 voices rose . . . from the midst of the forest." Likely this site was near the present Albeni Falls in Idaho on the Pend d'Oreille River. When the river became navigable in the spring, De Smet left for St. Mary's Mission on the Bitterroot where he spent Easter with the Flathead Indians.

No sooner than the snows melted, Father De Smet wrote, "In the beginning of February I set out to visit our different settlements and stations and to form new ones among the neighboring tribes of our reductions." He descended the Clark Fork River in the spring flood in a frail canoe to the Kalispell camp. With Father Hoecken and the tribal chiefs, he examined sites proposed for a permanent station. A cave located nearby he believed with little effort could be fitted out for a chapel. He named it "New Manresa" in honor of the first "Manresa cave" of Saint Ignatius in Spain. Father Hoecken was left here to develop the new Mission of St. Ignatius. Father De Smet again crossed the mountains to the Colville Valley and boarded a canoe at Kettle Falls destined for headquarters on the Willamette and in five days he reached Fort Vancouver. Here Father De Smet, as the superior, had administrative duties to care for, reports to make and he had also to confer with Vicar General F.N. Blanchet.

RETURN TO THE INTERIOR

After making all the purchases he believed necessary, in the late spring Father De Smet with Brother McGean and two helpers with eleven pack horses loaded with plows, spades, scythes, axes and carpenters' tools headed inland. "Our path was strewn with the whitened bones of horses and oxen, melancholy testimonies of miseries endured by other travelers . . . We passed the foot of Mount Hood . . . We were twenty days going from the Willamette to Walla Walla.'' By the second week of July the pack train had reached Lake Pend d'Oreille.

The Indian grapevine indicated that from eight to nine hundred Indians of various tribes were gathered at Kettle Falls for salmon fishing. Father De Smet immediately headed down the Pend d'Oreille River to the ''Flowery Trail'' and over to the Indian camps. ''I was received by my dear Indians with filial joy and tenderness. I caused a little chapel of boughs to be reared on an eminence, in the midst of the Indian huts''. The Colville Mission of St. Paul at Kettle Falls was thus started by Father De Smet. Father Ravalli later built a temporary chapel and in 1847 the present standing large log church and mission residence was constructed by Father Joset.

Having met the Lake Indians (Gens de lac) at Kettle Falls Father De Smet made a short excursion north to the Lake country, to their tribal grounds. He here established St. Peter's Mission Station. Later this station was visited by Father Nobili and then by a priest from St. Ignatius at the Kalispells.

The Kootenays and Flatbows were tribes never previously visited by a priest. In 1845 De Smet headed north to their country from Tobacco Plains where he had dedicated a mission to the Immaculate Heart of Mary. He went from present Bonner's Ferry into British Columbia as far as Cranbrook. On the Feast of the Assumption Father celebrated Mass for the Kootenays, erected a cross on the prairie and named this station ''The Assumption.'' The Kootenay or Araca-a-Plats and the Flatbows were of the Shalzi linguistic nation.

TO THE BLACKFEET

In the Bitter Root Valley the Blackfoot Indians continued to menace the converted Flatheads at St. Mary's Mission. So Father De Smet decided to go among the Blackfoot Indians to try to bring about peace. These Indians lived in the areas on both sides of the later international boundary. The territory was still jointly held by Britain and the United States. (The boundary treaty was signed June 1846). De Smet traveled up the Kootenay River passed the lakes at the source of the Columbia River, to the Vermillion River, then across the Continental Divide to the source of the Saskatchewan to the Hudson's Bay post, the Rocky Mountain House. From here he went south in search of the Blackfoot Indians, but winter snows hindered his search. Then he went north (lat. 55° 30′) to Fort Augustus (Edmonton) where he saw the New Year arrive. When spring came he left for Fort Assiniboine on the Athabaska River, going by dogsled, traveling on the ice of the river, to Fort Jasper. On April 25th he left to go over the mountains to Boat Encampment on the Big Bend of the Columbia River. By boat he went down to Fort Colvile getting there by the end of May and then proceeding down to the Jesuit House on the Willamette. This hazardous journey in mid-winter is described much in detail in De Smet's letters. He tells too, how frustrated he was in not reaching the Blackfoot Indians.

AGAIN TO EUROPE

On reviewing the needs of the missions Father De Smet decided again to go to Europe. In July he started up the Columbia River with supplies destined for the interior missions. In eight days the barge reached Fort Walla Walla. Then procuring horses, the pack train headed north to the Spokane River on the old Indian trail which passed Sprague Lake up to Tshimakain Mission, then up the Colville Valley to the "Flowery Trail". After a "march of eight hours" over the Selkirk Mountains they arrived at the

Kalispell Mission on the Pend d'Oreille. Father Hoecken's mission now had some eighteen buildings and about 500 Kalispels living in the "reduction". July 27th De Smet bade farewell to the Kalispels and headed for the Coeur d'Alene Mission. He was met there by Fathers Joset and Point, the two Jesuit Brothers and all the natives of the area. After a week here De Smet, Father Point and some natives left for St. Mary's Mission following the present Coeur d'Alene and St. Regis Rivers. "So tortuous indeed is its course here, that in less than eight hours we crossed it no less than forty-four times."

Accompanied by Father Point, De Smet after a week's sojourn with the Flathead Indians, left St. Mary's Mission August 16 heading east for the Blackfoot country. They left through Hell Gate and up the Deer Lodge River following some Flatheads on to the Yellowstone River. After the Flathead Indians defeated the Crows in a pitched battle some Blackfoot Indians met De Smet and admired openly his "medicine" which they believed helped the Flatheads to victory. The warring Blackfeet after the battle led De Smet easterly to meet the rest of their tribe. This was definitely in answer to his desires and prayers. The group kept getting larger as more Piegans, Bloods, Gros Ventres and others joined. By September 16th it was estimated over two thousand Indians were in the train. A Grand Council was held after five weeks of his stay among the Blackfeet and De Smet witnessed a "solemn peace" between the previous, treacherous enemies, a peace which did not endure too long. On September 28th Father De Smet boarded a barge for the long journey to St. Louis. Father Point remained at Fort Benton that winter with the Blackfoot Indians. From there he was sent to Canada and never returned.

Father De Smet's position as superior of the Rocky Mountain Missions was terminated with his return to St. Louis in 1846. In 1851 he was invited to the Great Council, thirty miles east of Fort Laramie at Horse Creek. The council lasted eighteen days in which

De Smet's influence brought peace and harmony to the Indians. After this excursion he spent seven years in routine duties as a procurator to the Jesuit order. May 15, 1858 he was given a commission as a Chaplain to General William S. Harney's troops for the Utah expedition. When he returned to St. Louis he offered his resignation to the army but it was rejected.

IN THE NORTHWEST AS CHAPLAIN

The interior Indian Wars of the Cayuse, Coeur d'Alenes, Spokanes and Yakimas had been put down by Colonel George Wright. However, unrest still filled the air. General William Harney, now Commander of the Northwest Department requested the services of Father De Smet. He sailed from New York by way of Panama on September 20, 1858 for Vancouver, Washington. As soon as he arrived it was decided that under orders he depart for the various tribes to visit the Indians, reconcile them and bring back representatives for a peace conference. He went then to the United States army Fort Walla Walla where he met several Coeur d'Alene and Spokane families, the hostages Colonel Wright had taken two months previously. They were well-provided for but still in captivity. Father De Smet arranged through General Harney for their release. "At my request the excellent commandant of the fort . . . set at liberty all the prisoners and hostages, both Coeur d'Alenes and Spokans, and he entrusted them to my charge to bring them on their way and return to their respective nations. These good Indians, particularly the Coeur d'Alenes had given the greatest edification to the soldiers during their captivity." (New Indian Sketches, p. 88)

Father De Smet spent the winter at the Coeur d'Alene Mission. He visited again the Flathead Mission, St. Ignatius, moved here now from the Kalispel lands. On April 16 he left for Fort Vancouver gathering the Indian chiefs for the peace conference. In the *New Indian Sketches* he names the Chiefs he gathered: Alexander of the Pend d'Oreilles, Victor of the Kalispells, Adolphus and Francis Saxa (Iroquois) of the Flatheads, Denis of the Chaudieres, Andrew Seltice and Bonaventure of the Coeur d'Alenes, Garry of the Spokanes, Kamiakin of the Yakimas. Chief Kamiakin when at Fort Walla Walla became unnerved and deserted the group. Father De Smet had spent a month gathering the chiefs together. Major Owen, an Indian Agent from the Bitterroot Valley, claimed superior authority over the priest-chaplain and interferred at Fort Walla Walla. De Smet diplomatically handled the situation to keep the Indian delegation at peace and General Harney was satisfied. Meeting with the General and the Indian department officer, with understatement Father De Smet wrote: "the conference produced most happy results on both sides." This meeting settled the tense conditions and peace came to the interior, except for the later flare-up of the Chief Joseph War of the Nez Perce in 1877.

While still at Fort Vancouver Father De Smet submitted his resignation to the army. General Harney accepted it June 1, 1859 and then De Smet started east over the mountains visiting the various Indian nations he had not seen for a number of years. He left Fort Benton on the Missouri in a small swift boat and on September 23rd he landed at St. Louis.

The "Charismatic Peace-maker" never again visited the plateau Pacific Northwest. He died at St. Louis University Jesuit House on May 23, 1873.

Edward J. Kowrach
Veradale, Washington
August 1984

CHECK-LIST OF EDITIONS OF *NEW INDIAN SKETCHES*

The original was written in French and translated into English by Robert A. Bakewell of St. Louis, Missouri.

1863—D. & J. Sadlier Co. of Boston.
1865—Sadlier Co. New York.
1870—Sadlier Co. New York.
1885—Sadlier Co. New York.
1886—Sadlier Co. New York.
1895—Kennedy, New York.
1904—Kennedy, New York.
1905—Chittendon & Richardson (used 1865 ed.)
1971—Shorey, Seattle, Washington (facsimile)
1984—Ye Galleon Press, Fairfield, Washington.

P. Vande Staene

The Cross of Peace—1845
The Source of the South Branch of the Saskatchewan River

PREFACE

The holy life of Catharine Tehgahkwita, the saintly virgin of the Mohawk, is well known; and the odor of her virtues is still fresh on the banks of the St. Lawrence, where she edified all by her life, and aided so many after her death. Among the sketches of Father De Smet, published recently in Belgium, is a short memoir of Louise Sighouin, a holy woman of the tribe of the Coeur-d'Alenes, which shows us another example of high sanctity attained in an Indian wigwam, and affords us a model and a patron through whom we may piously expect that God will grant favors for the glory of his servant and the salvation of souls. The biography is one that cannot fail to touch and instruct all.

To it we have added some of the more recent sketches of the pious missionary, whose letters are always so much esteemed, and a catechism of the Flathead Indians, to give some idea of the mode of instruction adopted by our missionaries, and the difficulty inherent in all the Indian languages of expressing religious thoughts. The illustrations in this work are from drawings by Father Point, whose pencil has preserved so many scenes and characters of the Rocky Mountains. They are the Baptism of Louise, and her venerated Grave.

S.

[Original preface printed in the 1886 D. & J. Sadlier edition.]

Sketch of LOUISE SIGHOUIN, in front of historic Old Sacred Heart Mission of the Coeur d'Alene Tribe, 1850, near Cataldo, Idaho—Idaho's oldest building.

by Coeur d'Alene artist, Lawrence Aripa, of Aripa Indian Arts, Plummer, Idaho.

LOUISE SIGHOUIN,

AN INDIAN WOMAN OF THE COEUR-D'ALENE TRIBE,

WHO DIED IN THE ODOR OF SANCTITY IN 1853

CHAPTER I.

CHILDHOOD AND BAPTISM OF LOUISE.

LOUISE SIGHOUIN, of the tribe of Skizoumish or Coeur-d'Alenes, daughter of the chief of the tribe, was endowed with the noblest qualities of mind and heart, which won her the esteem and respect not only of all her nation, but also of the neighboring tribes and of all whites who had an opportunity of knowing her. A poor and humble child, but rich in virtue and exalted in grace, Louise flowered in the desert like a lily amid thorns. She was an oasis amid a sterile waste; she was a light amid the shades of death. Like the poor woman in the Gospel, she had sought and found the lost treasure, and she carefully preserved it all the days of her life to her latest breath.

Before her baptism, even, she was remarkable for her rare modesty and reserve, great gentleness, and a solid judgment. Her words were everywhere listened to with admiration and pleasure, and her company sought in all families.

In October, 1841, a new era was preparing for her. In the course of the missions which I was then giving in the upper parts of the Rocky Mountains, I met for the first time three families of

Coeur-d'Alenes, returning from the bison hunt on the plains of the upper Missouri. They joined my little band, and we travelled together. I found them mild, affable, polite in disposition, and above all very eager for the word of God. For several consecutive days I conversed with them on different points of faith and on the Church. After an instruction on the importance and necessity of baptism, they earnestly implored me to grant that favor to three of their little children. They were the first fruits of this tribe. When these families parted with us, all testified the most lively gratitude for what they had heard and learned with happiness: they assured me that the whole tribe would willingly accept the beautiful word of the Great Spirit, which I had announced to them, and they gave me a most pressing invitation to visit them at the earliest moment in order to instruct them.

Six months after, in April, 1842 I proceeded to their quarters. My good Coeur-d'Alenes, who had been my travelling companions, had admirably prepared the way for my visit, and infused into all their countrymen an eager desire to hear the good tidings of the Gospel. In consequence of the account which they gave, the chiefs had already hastened to depute to St. Mary's Mission several young men, selected from the most intelligent, in order to ask for missionaries to instruct them in the holy truths of religion.

The tidings of my coming soon spread through all the country. The Indians were to be seen flocking from all sides, through forest and plain, by the rivers and the great lake, to meet me, and hear the law of God from the very lips of a Black Gown. My visit, consequently, had the most beneficial results. I baptized all the little children in the tribe and a good number of adults, who had hastened with holy avidity to come and receive the mustard seed mentioned in the Gospel.

Among these was good Louise Sighouin. Enlightened by a special grace, and wishing to turn to the glory of God and the good of souls the rank which she occupied and the universal esteem she had acquired in the whole tribe, she used all her influence to induce a great number of families to follow her to the rendezvous, which was the great Lake Coeur-d'Alene, in order to hear there the good and consoling word of the Gospel. From the very first she showed the greatest avidity for it; at all times was she most assiduous at the instructions of the missionary. Aided by his advice and counsels, she was seen advancing with a sure and rapid step, zealously and fervently in the path that was later to lead her to Christian perfection. Regenerated in the holy waters of baptism, where she received the name of Louise, she seemed to have reached the summit of her desires, and to think only of wearing unsullied the white robe which she had received, of keeping well trimmed on earth the flaming light that she had held in her hands, and of which from that moment she had seemed to realize and comprehend the sublime significance; in fine, of showing herself faithful and grateful to God for the great favors which he had deigned to grant to her.

Coeur d'Alene Lake

CHAPTER II.

LOUISE'S ZEAL FOR THE CONVERSION OF HER TRIBE AND HER STRUGGLES WITH THE MEDICINE-MEN.

SOON after this she resolved to devote herself entirely to the service of the missionaries who had come to labor in the territory of the Coeur-d'Alenes. With this view she generously renounced her native spot, the guidance of her father, the society of her relatives and acquaintances, to be with the missionaries at the first, and then at the second mission station established in those countries. "I will follow the Black Gowns," she often said, "to the end of the world, for fear that death should surprise and strike me far from them, and thus deprive me of the help of the holy sacraments, and the salutary counsels of the Fathers. I wish to profit by their presence and their instructions to learn to know the Great Spirit well, to serve him faithfully, and to love him with all my heart."

This desire, or rather this ardent thirst to hear the word of Eternal Life, never for a moment diminished in Louise. Sooner than be wanting to the fidelity of her promises and her pious resolutions, she subjected herself, with unlimited confidence in God and with a holy ardor, to the severest trials and greatest sacrifices. From the time of her conversion, during the whole residue of her life, she lived by choice and predilection in great poverty and in privations of every kind, never seeking to diminish them by the assistance of others, and without ever letting the slightest murmur escape her, As St. Paul lays it down, she seemed to profess "to know only Jesus

Christ, and him crucified."

The zeal and fervor in the service of God, which she manifested immediately after her baptism, were the unfailing tokens of a predestined soul, filled with extraordinary gifts from heaven. These privileged favors were manifested in all their light by her admirable gentleness, which the greatest opposition could not disturb, by her patience under every trial, by her truly angelic modesty, by her fervent and sustained piety. She seemed, as it were, absorbed in prayer, and nothing apparently could then distract her thoughts. Such was her avidity, her holy ardor, to hear the Word of God, that every time a new religious truth broke in its effulgence on her mind, a visible joy overspread her countenance and her whole person: to her it was the precious discovery of a hidden treasure, a living fountain to quench her thirst of heavenly truths, a bread of life giving her new vigor. Each time she sought to share her happiness, this bread, this fountain, this treasure, with all who were like her hungering for the divine Word.

An ardent and an untiring zeal for the salvation of souls seemed ever to occupy her thoughts. She employed all her leisure moments in the conversion and instruction of numerous pagans in her village. Neither the opposition which she encountered, nor the obstacles which she met,nor the insults which she received, nor the dangers to which she exposed herself, naught could divert her from the holy work which she had resolved to accomplish. Thus each day was marked by some new triumph, by some new increase of the number of the children of God or of the catechumens.

Louise boldly attacked face to face, the most formidable and dangerous adversaries of religion; the ministers of Satan himself, the sorcerers or jugglers, commonly called among the Indians *medicine-men*, who by their impostures and diabolical arts, always impose on the simple and ignorant. They are the most deadly enemies whom the missionaries encounter, and must ever combat in the bosom of the Indian tribes. They never cease by tricks and calumnies and lies to throw obstacles in the way of the missionary and fetter the progress of religion. The presence of the priest is the more odious to them as they know that their private interest, their wealth, is at stake, and that their illicit gains will vanish and cease on the manifestation of religious truths. *Inde irae!* Hence, their hatred and resentment; hence, too, the incessant war they wage on the ministers of the true faith, and the persecutions they incessantly excite against them, whenever they can exercise sufficient influence over their adherents. And on what a people did they exercise their influence, before the arrival of our missionaries in their country!

Father Point, a missionary among the Coeur-d'Alenes from 1842 to 1846, wrote of them as follows, in a letter printed in 1848. These details prove the civilizing tendency and power of religion.

"Not a quarter of a century since, the Coeur d'Alenes were so hard-hearted, that to paint them to the life, the common sense of their first visitors found no expression more just than the singular name which they still bear; minds so limited, that while rendering divine worship to all the animals that they knew, they had no idea of the true God, nor of their soul, nor consequently of a future life; in fine, a race of men so degraded, that of the natural law, there survived among them only two or three very obscure notions, which few, very few attempted to reduce to practice. Yet it must be said to the credit of the tribe, that there were always in their midst elect souls, who never bent the knee to Baal. I know some, who from the very day when the true God was preached to them, never had to reproach themselves with the shadow of an infidelity."

Among these the most remarkable was our heroine, Louise. Rising above all human respect, she always followed the advice of the missionary. As long as the wily medicine-men existed, she untiringly opposed and exposed them. She boldly entered their lodges, and with or without their leave, spoke to them of the great truths of religion, alone true and divine, exhorting them to follow it, in order to avoid the terrible judgments of God, hell with its frightful torments. She did this with such energetic fortitude, and such peremptory arguments, that their obstinacy was shaken and their obduracy softened.

Endowed with a heart and a courage above her sex, Louise feared neither the sneers nor the threats of these deceitful and embittered charlatans. Accordingly, the Almighty blessed the efforts of this "valiant woman" of the wilderness, and always crowned them with such extraordinary success, that in a short time the medicine-men and their silly juggleries fell into complete contempt. "In fine," wrote Father Point again, "from Christmas to Candlemas, the missionary's fire was kept up with all that remained of the ancient "medicine." It was a beautiful sight to behold the principal supporters of it, with their own hands destroy the wretched instruments which hell had employed, to deceive their ignorance or give credit to their impostures. And in the long winter evenings, how many birds feathers, wolves' tails, feet of hinds, hoofs of deers, bits of cloth, wooden images, and other superstitious objects were sacrificed!

Among Louise's chief conquests, they especially mention the conversion of Natatken, one of the principal leaders of the idolatrous sect. He resisted stubbornly; but at last, touched by the good example of all the converts, and above all, by the exemplary life of Louise's family, with which he was connected by blood, he yielded to the earnest exhortations, the sweet and persuasive words of the young girl, and opening his heart to the grace of our Lord after having long been a rebel, he came like a timid lamb to the humble fold of the Good Shepherd. Louise devoted herself with the utmost care to the instruction of the new catechumen, and formed him to a kind of apostolic work in his tribe. Till then a great master of Indian sorcery, he listened to and followed her wise counsels and instructions with the docility of a child; and after all the necessary trials, Louise led him, humble and contrite, with his wife and children, to the feet of the priest, to receive the sacrament of regeneration. Natatken received the name of Isidore. He soon became very zealous and very fervent. Endowed with native eloquence, he unceasingly exhorted his companions to convert and persevere in the faith, and in the holy practices which religion imposes on her children. He gave the example himself. He remained faithful to the grace of the Lord till his death, which was as edifying as consoling.

Emotestsulem, one of the great chiefs of the tribe, after having been baptized under the name of Peter Ignatius, had unfortunately relapsed into gambling, the ordinary forerunner of apostasy among the Indians. As soon as Louise heard this sad news, although she was at a distance of two days' march, she resolved to go to his town and find him so as to endeavor to bring him back to his duties. She set before his eyes the scandal which his conduct occasioned in the tribe, the injustice of his course, and the danger to which he exposed his faith. She spoke to him with energy. Such was the authority that Louise had acquired by her great charity and exemplary life, such was the respect which she commanded from all, that the great chief hearkened to her with the submission of a child, and went to cast himself at the feet of the priest in the tribunal of penance, to repair the scandal and be reconciled to God.

These two incidents, the conversion of Natatken and that of Emotestsulem, will surprise all who know how reluctant the Indians, and especially their chiefs, are to receive correction, especially when it is administered by a woman.

Let us say a few words of the famous sect of jugglers or sorcerers, whom our modern spiritualists have begun to style mediums. This sect is spread over all the Indian tribes of both Americas, from the Esquimaux, who inhabit the Arctic regions, to the extremity of Patagonia.

All historians agree in saying, that the most perverse and wicked men in all the tribes are the medicine-men. Before their conversion to the faith, as well as everywhere else among the Indian tribes, each Coeur-d'Alene had his *manitou* (tutelary spirit or divinity). To this manitou the Indian addresses his prayer or supplication, and offers his sacrifices, when he is in any danger, sets out for war, or goes fishing or hunting, as well as in every other enterprise in which he is about to engage, in order to obtain success or some extraordinary favor. He believes that he can ask everything of his manitou, reasonable or unreasonable, good or bad. To obtain favors, he must be able to handle the bow and arrow, and although initiation to the manitou is considered as the most important act of life, the adept is required to submit to ceremonies and practices which are generally very difficult and often very painful. The young man after making profound incisions on the fleshy parts of the body, or after a rigorous fast, is supposed to discover in his dreams the form or resemblance under which the manitou manifests himself. During his whole life he is bound to bear the image or a mark of it; and on all occasions he must present his offerings and address his prayers to him. His talisman is the feather or beak of a bird, the claw or tooth of an animal, a root, a herb, a fruit, a scale, a stone, no matter what. He believes that this tutelary spirit will protect him against the evil genii, who to injure the children of earth excite the winds and waves, lightning, thunder, and storm. This spirit protects him against the attacks of his enemies, and wild beasts, and in all diseases that come upon him.

If I mention these dangerous and diabolical superstitions, so profoundly rooted in the mind of the Indian, it is to display more clearly the courage, firmness, patience, and perseverance which Louise must have had to oppose them successfully and even overcome them. Louise prepared herself for the struggle by long prayers and frequent fasts, and fortified herself by her humility, by her fidelity to the grace of our Lord, who made use of her as a chosen instrument to crush the monstrous serpent beneath her feet, and expel him from her tribe. Nevertheless, the devil never sleeps, he is always sowing tares in the good field, as Holy Scripture tells us, he "goeth about like a roaring lion, seeking whom he may devour." We must always fly to the "Watch and pray," for we perceive always that some trace of the old leaven remains.

Interior of the Old Mission of the Sacred Heart - Cataldo, Idaho

Photo: Will Hawkins

Indian Chief Proclaims the Buffalo Hunt
Indians reclining in their tents

CHAPTER III.

LOUISE'S ZEAL FOR THE INSTRUCTION OF HER TRIBE

AS I have already remarked, Louise manifested an ardent desire and an active perseverence in instructing herself in all that pertained to the word of God and the holy practices of religion. She sought in the first place to enrich her fair soul with heavenly truths, and then with admirable zeal and charity she endeavored to relieve the missionary in his laborious toils and the continual fatigue he encountered, especially in instructing old people and children. Entirely wrapped up in her noble calling, she would go several times in the day to the priest, to set forth her doubts and ask an explanation of them, and light on some points either in the prayers or in the catechism, which she wished to fathom more deeply.

This constant assiduity and application to the study of heavenly things, soon rendered her capable of being the head teacher of the catechism, and enabled her to instruct the underteachers with great fruit. At every explanation and development which she received from the missionary, she would say ingenuously, "I thank the Great Spirit for the beautiful alms which he has deigned to bestow on me," and she felt herself bound to impart her knowledge to all the catechumens, to make them partakers in her happiness. She set the example to those good mothers, of whom Father Point speaks in his letter, who, not satisfied with giving their children the food which they refused themselves, spent long evenings in breaking, not only to parents and friends, but also to strangers, eager to hear them, the bread of the divine word, gathered by them during the day. The missionary, sometimes present at the pious meetings of these good women, admired the spirit of God which animated them, and applied to them the promise of the prophet, "The Lord shall give the Word to them that preach good tidings with great power."—Ps. lxvii. 12. The patience and constancy which Louise displayed in the office of catechist, deserve the highest eulogy; the salvation of souls was a work of predilection to her; the hours of the day seemed too short to satisfy her zeal, and she often consumed a good part of the night instructing her neighbor.

Amid all her occupations and exertions for the good of others, Louise never neglected the care and ordering of her own house. Her prayers, her good works, her words, and her good example had drawn down the blessings of heaven on her poor and humble abode, and this model cabin, great by the virtues which it enshrined, shone with radiance amid all the other Indian lodges. Louise had comprehended at once and fully the whole extent of the duties of a good wife and mother, duties till then almost unknown to the Indians, among whom, from the moment of leaving childhood, each one becomes absolute master of himself and his actions. By her conduct beyond reproach, by her motherly vigilance over the behavior of her children, by the simple and persuasive gentleness with which she treated them on all occasions, Louise had inspired them with the most profound respect and entire confidence, and had so closely bound to her their tender hearts, that a desire manifested, or a single word from the lips of their good mother, was an absolute order, a law for them, which they accomplished in all its requirements with eagerness and joy.

Louise attended the divine offices with the greatest exactness. Although in delicate health and often sick, she never failed to be present at all the religious ceremonies in use in the Church; she attended Mass, morning and evening prayers, the expositions and benedictions of the Blessed Sacrament, and all the other practices of devotion. Her modesty, her recollectedness, and her fervent prayers, always served as an edifying example to all present. She seemed at the summit of her happiness and joy, every time that she was permitted to approach the holy table; her preparation and thanksgiving often took whole days.

In catechising and in church Louise fulfilled all the duties of parents to their children. Sitting in their midst, she watched over their conduct and their innocent bearing. Rarely was she severe; when there was anything to reprehend, the correction was always made with a mother's tenderness and goodness, which won her the hearts not only of the children but also of their parents. She merited and received from all the tribe the beautiful name of *good grandmother*. Her counsels and corrections were always and by all received with respect, submission, and gratitude; and the happy results were seen in a complete and blessed change of the whole tribe, thus augmenting joy and happiness in all hearts.

Louise, although the best instructed in the truths of religion, nevertheless came regularly to attend the catechetical instructions which the missionary was accustomed to give the children daily. She could be seen sitting or standing outside the half-opened door, regardless of the weather, heat or cold, rain or snow. She wished to gather all the important points of each instruction for her own spiritual good and that of others.

When there was a question of admitting an old man, a boy or girl to partake of the Sacraments, she prepared and instructed them for several days in her lodge, impressing them with the high importance of the grace which they were going to receive, and the happiness which they were going to enjoy. She then aided them with the greatest care to examine their conscience. And that nothing should be lacking in the preparations, she took them one by one to the tribunal of penance, telling them: "Here, kneel at the feet of the Father, who has the power to reconcile you to the Great Spirit. Say the Confiteor with a great sorrow for your offences. Confess your sins with profound humility.'' She would then withdraw to a short distance to wait for them, and then lead them to the foot of the altar to receive the spotless Lamb, and be nourished with the bread of angels. Louise did not leave them till they had finished their thanksgiving. She wished to supply in some sort the lack of memory or capacity, when the parties seemed to need it. For fear of being guilty of any grave omission, the chiefs themselves, and many of the most esteemed men in the nation, went regularly to have her assistance in preparing for a worthy reception of the Blessed Sacrament.

Among other pious practices introduced by Louise in the mission, we are indebted to her for the following. On solemn days, the night previous to the general communion, hymns are sung alternately, sometimes in one lodge and sometimes in another, with charming harmony. These pious canticles have reference to the approaching day, which they are preparing to celebrate worthily. On the eve of the communion, the Indians arrange their exterior, and for most this is now small affair. They wash, clean, and mend the clothes or rags which scarcely cover them; they go and bathe in a retired part of the river, even on Christmas Eve and when the water is freezing. Each one keeps in his leather bag, which serves as a wardrobe (for they have no chests or drawers), a piece of linen or white cotton, or a colored handkerchief; the women and girls wear them as a veil, the men as a cravat. Their toliet as you see is very simple and very poor, but each does his best, even outwardly, to come worthily and with respect to the table of the Lord.

CHAPTER IV.

LOUISE'S CHARITY FOR THE SICK.—HER POVERTY.

AMONG all the virtues which distinguished Louise and which she cherished and practised with so much zeal and ardor, shone forth especially her Christian charity to the sick and dying. Father Gazzoli, who has for many years directed that mission, assured me that during Louise's life, he never went to the bedside of a sick or dying person, without there meeting the Indian "Good Samaritan." She devoted herself to the continual service of the sick, and tended them with as much care, patience, and interest, as she could have bestowed on her own children and parents. While relieving their bodies with admirable and truly maternal charity, she never failed to think of their soul, and devoted herself with still greater zeal and fervor to heal its wounds, especially when the state of the patient's conscience seemed most to require it. She suggested pious thoughts, and recited with them acts of faith, hope, charity, contrition, resignation, and submission to the holy will of our Lord; she constantly exhorted them to have patience in their painful trials, in imitation of our Lord, who died on the cross to save us; in one word she faithfully served her God in the person of her neighbor, conformable to these words of the Gospel: "Amen, I say to you, as long as you did it to one of these, my least brethren, you did it to me."—Matt. xxv. 40. With no other recompense than what she expected from her divine Master, she fulfilled all the duties of an excellent nurse. This service she performed with as much exactness and devotedness, as an exemplary Sister of Mercy or Daughter of St. Vincent de Paul could have shown. On many occasions when she wished to exercise her voluntary mission of charity, she had to consent to great sacrifices, and almost heroic efforts over herself, to overcome her natural repugnance. Father Gazzoli relates that one day, according to his custom in certain circumstances, he invited Louise to accompany him to a patient, to aid him in the care which a most loathsome sore required. Such was the sight of the corrupt mass, that for the first time the repugnance of the courageous woman overcame her; she durst not touch it or do the least to dress it. The missionary perceived it, and opened the abscess himself. Some moments after, Louise expressed the most lively regret at having yielded to her feelings, and told him with humility and respect: "I am greatly ashamed, Father; my weakness got the better of me. I admire your charity. I lacked courage to imitate it." She atoned for what she had reproached herself with as a fault, and immediately began to nurse the sick man, and dressed his sore with the greatest assiduity for about two months, till he recovered. It was the first time, added Father Gazzoli, that good Sighouin shrunk from a charitable desire which he expressed, and it was the last. In the sequel and down to her death, under every circumstance, she continued to fulfil, with promptness and fidelity, the requests made by her pious director, and made by him to offer her occasions of victory and merit before God. She had completely triumphed over herself, and in her humble constancy at the bedside of the sick, the most loathsome cases seemed to her the most agreeable and attractive.

Amid Louise's noble acts of charity and patience, may be cited the care she took for several years of a poor child on whom all human miseries of mind and body seemed to accumulate. An orphan, destitute of every thing, crippled, blind, and what is worse, stubborn and ungovernable, such was Louise's adoptive child. Such a child was doubtless a rich windfall to exercise a saint. One day she told the missionary that she could not manage Ignatius (that was the orphan's name), and that he would not mind her in the least. The Father who supplied his food and clothing, thought that by threatening to make him fast, he might be reduced to submission; but when it was tried, Ignatius rolled up his shirt-sleeve, and showing his arm, said: "Look there, I am fat. I can fast." He was then eleven or twelve years old. Such was the disposition of the child on whom Louise lavished the care of a tender mother for several years, till God recalled the poor boy from this world.

Louise had a niece named Agatha, the only daughter of one of her sisters. She was, and justly so, her child of predilection. Pious, and ever attentive to her aunt's good advice and wise lessons, Agatha verified her name by her exemplary conduct, and by her example amid her young companions. She was well instructed in her catechism, and was preparing for her first communion; she had already presented herself at the tribunal of penance to make a good confession, when an attack of apoplexy deprived her of speech. She survived only one day, suffering greatly, but with admirable patience. Her death was a severe and painful trial to the heart of Louise, who long after still kept her loss fresh in her mind, yet she submitted perfectly to the divine will, and convinced that her niece had gone to a better world, she overcame her grief, and shed not a tear; on the contrary, she never ceased thanking the Almighty for the favor he had bestowed upon Agatha, by snatching her away from the dangers of earth to set her in his heavenly mansion.

Louise lived in great poverty; yet the slightest murmur never escaped her to show her wants or her suffering. When the missionary was able to give her any charity, he had first to ask her whether she was not in some need, either of food or clothing. She regarded as nothing the privations and voluntary poverty which she imposed on herself through love for her divine Lord, and for her neighbor. Her lodge, formed of flag-mats, stood beside the *house of prayer*, or church, and near the poor cabin of the missionaries. There in happiness and contentment Louise found all her treasure, all her joy, and the complete fulfilment of her pious desire. There she unceasingly contemplated the home of eternal rest, which the Lord has prepared for his elect in heaven, and to which he alludes in the words: "My kingdom is not of this world."—John, xviii. 36. Those which the Acts of the Apostles add: "In very deed, I perceive that God is not a respecter of persons. But in every nature, he that feareth him, and worketh justice is acceptable to him" (Acts, x. 34), seemed perfectly realized in poor Louise. From her conversion she faithfully followed the career which Providence had traced for her. Poverty with zeal and charity were her joy. Amid the poor of her tribe she may be said to have been the poorest, and always blessed God for her lot. Thus it is, that as we read in St. Mark, the "last shall be first." Sighouin fully comprehended this maxim, and she is at once a striking and consoling example of it. How glorious and beautiful is the society of fervent Christians, in all ranks and conditions of life! By its heavenly doctrines, benevolence admirably tempers authority; justice and charity reign in all hearts; the great humbles himself without derogating from his dignity, and the poor, the lowly, even the poor Indian woman, not only does not fall in contempt, but is elevated by the consideration of a common origin, the hope of a common end, and the distribution of the same means; in the sight of heaven all are equal, for all are children of one same Father, and called, though in different ways, to the possession of a common heritage.

Behold, then, the humble Louise, a poor Indian woman, an obedient, charitable, and submissive Christian. Zeal for souls, zeal for the house of God devours her. Endowed with heroic constancy and courage, she surmounts all obstacles that oppose her generous designs. Where does she find her courage, her strength, her consolation, her happiness, if not in the love of her God, in an entire confidence in him, and a holy indifference in regard to all else? All her actions seem to express constantly these words: "God alone for me! . . . God alone today and forever! . . . God alone for all eternity!" She devoted herself entirely to the cause of God; her labors, her troubles, her pain, will receive their reward. "She hath chosen the better part, which shall not be taken away from her."—Luke x. 42.

Interior of the Chapel Among the Coeur d'Alenes
(Before Father Ravalli's construction.)

CHAPTER V.

THE SPECIAL DEVOTION OF LOUISE TO THE CROSS OF OUR LORD, TO THE BLESSED SACRAMENT, AND TO THE SOULS IN PURGATORY.

LOUISE always manifested a great devotion to the Holy Cross. In the sowing season, in order to draw down God's blessing on the crop, she each year presented to her spiritual director the seed corn, to ask him to bless it. She then went through the great harvest field and the fields of the Indians, digging up a little piece of ground in the shape of a cross to plant her grain in. During the whole time that she maintained this practice, it was every year observed, that the crop was very abundant and very fine, even when the neighbors all around lost their grain. She had learned that heaven and earth had been disunited, and that the Cross had reconciled them; that no one can enter into heaven except by the way of the Cross. She sowed her grain in the form of a cross, having implicit confidence that our Lord, who died on the cross, would fructify it. The Cross was her refuge on earth; it was her strength and consolation till death. We may here repeat those beautiful words of the venerable Bishop Challoner: "Jesus is delivered into the hands of his executioners; his suffering, his ignominy begins; he dies on an infamous gibbet; and he is no sooner lifted up, than *he draws all things to him.* The Cross dispels the darkness that covered the face of the earth: it unveils the great mystery of life and death, of God, of our duties and our eternal destiny; in a word, in all that till then had been hidden from the wisest of pagan antiquity. The Cross teaches us to suffer for the cause of justice, to bear wrongs for the glory of God, to die for his love. How admirably has the Gospel been styled by St. Paul *the word of the Cross.*"

Louise had a tender devotion to the most Blessed Sacrament of the altar. That great mystery of the love of God, who deigns to lower, and as it were, annihilate himself, and "whose delight is to be with the children of men" (Prov., viii. 31), seemed to touch the good Indian woman most profoundly, and to fill her heart with the liveliest gratitude. Every morning she attended the holy sacrifice of the Mass with the greatest recollectedness. For a long time she went regularly to the missionary's cabin to ask explanations and instructions on the Holy Sacrament of the altar, without his supposing it to result from any motive but a desire of instruction. It was not till after the death of Louise, that he learned that when she had fully comprehended the meaning and seen the explanation of the principal ceremonies and rubrics in the celebration of the most holy mystery, she composed short prayers, full of unction, like those found in our best prayer books. I must remark here that this practice was then as yet unknown by the catechumens among the Indians, for the missionaries, especially in the first years that followed the establishement of the mission, were unable to go beyond the most elementary instructions on the points of doctrine of the most absolute necessity. But the zeal of Louise was by no means limited to her own soul; she had at the same time in view the spirtual good and advancement of her neighbor by all these holy practices. Gifted with an excellent memory, she communicated with care and eagerness to others all the instructions that she had received on the holy sacrifice of the Mass. The beautiful and admirable little prayers of which I have just spoken were in harmony with the different parts of the Mass, perfectly conformable to the spirit of the Church, full of sense and piety; they seemed dictated under the inspiration of the divine Master. We may say with all assurance and truth, that this useful work of Louise was far beyond the ordinary capacity and reach of a poor Indian.

Among the holy practices in which Louise displayed most zeal, fervor, and charity, and which always seemed dearest to her, all remarked her great devotion for the souls in purgatory. All her prayers, all her actions, all the merits that she might obtain from God by her pious and active life, were directed to this noble intention. She succeeded, too, after persevering efforts, in making the whole tribe relish and adopt her beautiful devotion. Every day, even during the rigorous season of winter, she proceeded to the cemetery to spend some time there in prayer. When the household occupations of her poor family prevented her visiting it by day, she went there late in the evening, or even during the night. This was frequently the case. It seems that hell endeavored to raise obstacles to prayers so agreeable to heaven, and, at the same time, deprive the souls in purgatory of so many suffrages, and good Sighouin of all the merits she daily laid up for herself. The fact was this. Before relating it, I must observe that, in the whole tribe, Louise was regarded as a brave and nowise timid woman, and that on many occasions she gave unequivocal proofs of her natural courage. And yet it several times happened that when at prayer in the cemetery she would be seized with affright, at the sight of fantastic figures that she seemed to behold before her. Once the spectres appeared in so frightful a manner, that, trembling with fear, she ran back to the camp with loud cries. The men immediately all flew to arms, as though a powerful enemy had assailed the village. All were convinced that the alarm given by Louise must have a real foundation. Father Gazzoli, who relates the facts, had much trouble in restoring order and tranquillity in the camp; he succeeded however, by promising to act as sentinel all night over his dear Indians. The next day he recommended Louise not to be disturbed in her prayers by the influence of such fears; and in case the phantoms returned again to molest her, to come, even though it were midnight, and tell him, but no one else, so as to create a panic in the village. On this occasion as ever, she showed her obedience and submission; and although the frightful visions returned from time to time, her victory over the demon was complete. From that time for several years, and down to the period of her last illness, she calmly continued her pious visits to the cemetery, exempt from all trouble and all fear. One day the missionary in an instruction advised his flock to remember the souls in purgatory, especially after communion. Louise received the recommendation as an advice from heaven, and the first time she approached the holy table, she was seen, after receiving the Blessed Sacrament, proceeding to the cemetery at the head of all the communicants, where they spent a considerable time in prayer for the relief of the faithful departed. Her example greatly increased this beautiful practice of Christian life; the greatest part of the Indians were soon seen following their pious guide to the place of rest; at last all went. This holy custom is still observed.

CHAPTER VI.

LOUISE'S PENITENTIAL SPIRIT: HER HORROR OF SIN, AND ZEAL TO PRESERVE OTHERS FROM IT.

OUR poor Indians have a very limited intelligence; their progress in religious instruction is very slow, retarded especially by the difficulty which the missionaries encounter in the language of the Indians, which is very rich to express whatever is material; but excessively poor in all that relates to the explanation of spiritual things. Hence, it happens that many of these poor people have not yet that salutary horror and shame for sin, which are so powerful a means to restrain men's passions. Thus a woman who has been unfaithful or rebellious to her husband will receive pardon the moment she shows sorrow for it. A man who has grossly insulted another, or done him a grievous wrong, will go and smoke the calumet of peace with the injured person, or enter his lodge, or give him an equivalent for the wrong committed. These reparations are generally received, and considered sufficient, and the offender recovers the good graces of the injured party. "The wound is covered," as they express it; that is to say, "All is forgotten." When any one commits a fault, secret or notorious, he goes of his own accord to present himself to the chief and ask to be whipped. "The whip has covered his fault," no one can then speak of it. The missionary has sometimes to instruct them in the confessional on this point; for the penitent would come, and not accuse himself of grievous faults known to the whole tribe. In vain will the confessor say: "You have been guilty of such or such a sin, you must accuse yourself of it before God." The penitent will reply: "Pardon, Father, I went to the chief, and the sin you mention was covered by the whip; the whip has covered my fault." I mention this usage of the Coeur-d'Alenes, because our good Louise sometimes presented herself to the chief to be publicly whipped. But here the case was different; she seized the opportunity in a spirit of profound humility, always regarding herself as a poor and enormous sinner, and at the same time from a desire to satisfy her devotion to imitate our Lord, by submitting to the cruel flagellation. Louise's faults were only of the nature of those of which the Book of Proverbs speaks, when he says that the "just man shall fall seven times and shall rise again."—Prov. xxiv. 16. Nevertheless, what she called her faults, caused her such regret and confusion, that the missionary often found her bathed in tears. At the least fault, her contrition was so lively, and, at the same time, her veneration for the *Lodge of the Lord* (the church) so profound, and her respect for the cabin of the priest so sincere, that she durst not enter either till she had approached the tribunal of penance. We admired in her, too, that faith and that love of God, which, in the real sins and faults of others, made her share in their sorrow and shame.

A certain member of the tribe, blinded by passion, in spite of all the obstacles in the way of his illicit desires, had resolved to unite himself with a near relative of Louise's, and who was at the same time nearly related to himself. Among the Indians there is no power to prevent evil in such a case but argument; when this fails there is no means to which they can have recourse. The wretched man, deaf to all the advice of the chief and of his own friends, obdurately closing his ears to the exhortations of the missionary, had united himself to the object of his desires. The traits which I have already given of the pure soul of Louise, will speak sufficiently the grief and bitterness which this depravity in a near kinswoman must have caused her. She had already employed all the means of persuasion in her power, to prevent the union of these two miserable people. They had turned a deaf ear to her wholesome advice and counsel, as to all that others had offered. One day the pastor showed himself more than ordinarily troubled and afflicted at the depravity and obstinacy of his two lost sheep and at the great scandal they gave the whole tribe. He said publicly and vehemently, "We must put a stop to this at once. Let each one then implore the divine assistance, and beg the Almighty, that with as little delay as possible, he will aid to remove this great scandal from among us." Louise was present and heard the missionary's words. She was ignorant of the guilty man's threats, for he had resolved to repel by brute force and by arms, whoever would dare to prevent his retaining the object of his guilty love. Invested with courage above her strength, like the strong woman in the Scriptures, and full of confidence in God, brave Sighouin immediately started from the village over woods and mountains, and marched for several days to the spot where the two culprits had hidden themselves to hide their crime and infamy. She entered the lodge to the great surprise of the guilty pair. One rushed at her, whip in hand, the other threatened to strike her; but Louise addressed them on the misfortune of their state, in words so resolute, so energetic, so overwhelming, that they stood silent and confounded before her, and without difficulty she rescued from his hands the woman whom sin alone had made his partner. She took her to her own house, and kept her there till a dispensation was obtained, on which they were lawfully married. The charity and zeal of Louise aided from on high, thus came forth triumphant from a struggle as heroic as it was delicate.

In another and nearly similar case, a wretched man drew his

dagger to strike Louise, while loading her with insulting words and terrible threats; but the Christian heroine, with a calm and serene brow, portrayed to him the enormity of his conduct, his ingratitude to God, the scandal given to his neighbor. "I have come here," she said, "for the honor of God, and the salvation of your soul; I fear nothing." Here below, life is but a short passage. "The world passeth away," says the beloved Apostle, "and the concupiscence thereof. But he that doth the will of God abideth forever."—1 John, ii. 17. Louise fully comprehended these maxims, she never shrunk from any danger when the glory of the Almightly was concerned.

Louise paid special attention to the young girls of her tribe. She took care of their religious instruction, and diligently watched over their behavior. In the absence of their parents she made them all lodge in her cabin of mats, and took the entire direction of them. To understand this, it will be necessary to make a little digression. An Indian lodge of mats is a pretty commodious, though not very attractive abode. It assumes all dimensions, according to the number of persons to be accommodated; a few more poles and mats are added, and the arrangements are completed. Thus Louise was able to make room for a considerable number of beds for the children, for each one has her blanket or buffalo-robe. Their tables are the bare ground. Their dishes, plates, and spoons, are pieces of bark or wood; their fingers serve for forks and their teeth for knives. It takes an Indian, at most, half an hour to change a lodge into a large hostelry, and furnish it to correspond. Thus Louise was able to see herself at the head of a numerous household who were her delight. How beautiful it was to comtemplate the good Indian Grandmother tenderly loved and respected, amid her cherished children!

CHAPTER VII.

SICKNESS AND DEATH OF LOUISE.

WE may apply to Louise the beautiful words of the Scriptures: "Being made perfect in a short space, he fulfilled a long time."—Wisdom, iv. 13. After her vocation to the faith, she did not indeed live long years on the earth, but her years were full of merits before God. "She walked in the ways of the Lord with a rapid step." In all that she did, she constantly kept her eyes fixed on her heavenly home, awaiting those eternal goods of which the great Apostle speaks; she made noble efforts, and employed all her moments to embellish and enrich her soul with all Christian virtues. By her regular attendance at the instructions, by her constant spirit of prayer, by the practice of every species of good work, she increased more and more in the grace and knowledge of our Lord and sweet Saviour, Jesus Christ.

Her last illness left her the use of all her faculties, which she preserved to her last breath. She thus prepared for death with all the tranquillity of the just. Her prayer was fervent and uninterrupted, her patience superior to every trial. Entirely taken up with the salvation of her soul, she seemed utterly unmindful of the sufferings of her body; she sought no relief, and never betrayed the least sign of impatience; she often tenderly kissed the cross, which she always carried around her neck. The desire of the Apostle "to be dissolved and to be with Christ'' (Phil. i. 23), seemed to be during her illness her only motto and her only preoccupation.

''Always at the bedside of her who had so greatly aided me in my visits to the sick, and who had always served as my interpreter, and given me her aid with the ignorant,—the spiritual directress, the guardian angel of her whole tribe,—I had the happiness to witness this touching scene.'' says Father Gazzoli, the spiritual director of Louise. ''Her virtues had shone like a brilliant torch amid the Indians; she had never sullied the white robe of innocence which she had received in baptism. I witnessed the great power of the Cross, which displayed in the desert virtues till then unknown which produces wherever it is planted so many holy martyrs, so many confessors, so many virgins and illustrious penitents. Here, amid these isolated mountains, appears a poor Indian woman, whose unshaken faith and firm hope render her superior to trials of every kind. I desired to relieve her in some way; she in obedience gratefully received what I offered, yet without seeking or asking the slightest relief or the slightest mitigation of her pains, which she accepted as so many special graces of our Lord.''

Louise received from the hands of the minister of God all the consolations of the Church, the Holy Viaticum especially, with truly angelic piety and consolation. She thanked our Lord in all the humility of her soul, for the great favors which he deigned to grant her in that last hour of her earthly anguish, committing to his holy Providence her crippled husband and beloved children. She then made an effort to rally her little remaining strength, to thank her spiritual director for all the care which he constantly lavished on her, and especially in his instructions; she especially commended to his spirtual care the charge of all her family. The words which Louise addressed to her husband and her grieving children were consoling, full of trust in God's divine and paternal goodness, full of resignation to His holy will, and of firm hope to be one day all united again in their heavenly home. At last she turned to those who surrounded her death bed, happy witnesses of all these edifying scenes, which the just dying in the Lord present to the living, and which realize the words of Holy Writ: "Blessed are the dead who die in the Lord."—Apoc. xiv. 13. She begged those around to intone in their language the touching hymn in honor of the souls in purgatory, and accompanied it herself in a feeble and dying voice scarcely perceptible. They were still singing it when Louise, unperceived by any, slept calmly in our Lord.

Her beautiful soul had taken its heavenward flight. She happily left the place of trouble, misery, and death, to pass to an abode of glory and peace, the delights whereof are eternal. In her were fulfilled what St. James teaches us when he says: "Blessed is the man that endureth temptation, for when he hath been proved, he shall receive the crown of life, which God hath promised to them that love him."—St. James, i. 12. In the pleasing hope that henceforth the eternal crown is her lot, with the deep-seated trust in her power with God, we addressed to her in heaven our poor prayers: "O Louise, intercede with God for him who conferred baptism on you, and was your spiritual director; for your husband, for your children, and for all your dear Skizoumish. Obtain for us all the grace of perseverance in the holy service of our Lord. Amen."

I (Fr. Gazzoli) then addressed those around:

"Skizoumish! the example of the pious Sighouin is in your midst, we must profit by it. Henceforth she belongs to the whole nation, for she is the common beloved mother. As we all one day desire to share the glorious reward which she has just obtained by her virtues and good works, we must all follow the path which she has traced for us, and which leads to everlasting happiness. From the day of her baptism, in April, 1842, she constantly, night and day, devoted herself to your instruction. In the service of her God, she accepted with joy and eagerness, the privations, misery, contradictions, which it pleased Him to send her. In her this day are verified the words of the Lord addressed to the just: 'Because thou hast kept the word of my patience, I will also keep thee from the hour of temptation, which shall come upon the whole world to try them that dwell upon the earth.' "—Apoc. iii. 10.

The death of Louise Sighouin was the signal of a sudden desolation and a universal grief in the tribe, which lost a mother beloved by all, and especially by the children, a faithful friend to the whole nation, the comfort of the sick and afflicted, a guide and a support! The loss was immense, we avow. Yet this mourning was that of a Christian people, and not that of a perverse and unbelieving world, that has no hope beyond the grave. Amid this Indian tribe was renewed the salutary sadness that we ordinarily admire at the death of the just, whose memory is ever dear and in benediction, according to the words of the Holy Ghost: "O how beautiful is the chaste generation with glory: for the memory thereof is immortal: because it is known both with God and with men." Wisdom, iv. 1.

The minister of the Lord was still reciting the last prayers of the Church, invoking the angels and saints to receive the soul of her who had just expired, to present it at the throne of the Most High, when one of these kneeling beside him, ran out crying: "Sighouin, good Sighouin is dead!" The cry was taken up and echoed in the valley and in the foot of the high mountains which encircle the Residence of the Sacred Heart. The Indians ran up in crowds around the lodge of the departed. In their impatience to gratify their desire of gazing once more on the pious woman, the lodge was invaded, but it was too small to hold them all, the mats were torn from the poles; the lodge thus opened on all sides, enabled the crowd of spectators to satisfy their pious wish, and they gazed in admiring silence on the last sleep of Louise.

It is a custom of the Indians for the relatives and friends of a deceased person to assemble in his lodge after his death. When the missionary, after reciting the prayers of the Church, leaves the lodge, he says: "Pray, my children, for the repose of his soul," and adds some words suited to the circumstances. Then, on a signal from one of the nearest relatives of the deceased, all present burst into tears and groans, either real or feigned, or rather they begin lamentations, often forced, and extorted rather by the usual ceremony, than by a real sorrow caused by the loss of the deceased. On Louise's death the scene of mourning was far different: it was doubtless sincere. Father Gazzoli thus relates it: "I was an eyewitness, moved to tears by all that passed. My emotion kept increasing, especially when, even before the end of the prayers, universal cries, and tears, interrupted by sobs, announced clearly that no ceremony was enacting here, but on the contrary, they had assembled to pay a just tribute of gratitude and admiration to Louise's virtues, and to relieve the lively grief caused by her loss."

It must not be imagined that sunset, on this as on other occasions, put an end to these demonstrations of sorrow, regret, veneration, and love, displayed over the mortal remains of good Louise: they rather increased. The Indians immediately put up a vast lodge, which they illuminated by a fire of resinous wood. The body, becoming wrapped in skins of wild animals, was respectfully laid upon a bed of straw; a great number watch around, and recite prayers aloud during the whole night. The pious ceremonies of that night were till then unexampled in the country of the Coeur-d'Alenes. There was on this occasion a most touching, edifying, and extraordinary unanimity. Men, women, and children, were seen surrounding with equal eagerness the corpse of Louise, unable to tear themselves from her whom they called by so many titles, their *mother,* their *guide*, and their *true friend.* Their prayers and hymns were from time to time interrupted by edifying discourses on the life and heroic virtues of the deceased; the principal chiefs of the nation were the first to retrace most touching pictures of them for the assembly.

The missionary, struck at the spectacle of so striking a

testimony borne to virtue by a people possessed of such feeble ideas of it, believed it his duty to go and preside in this pious assembly. He proceeded to the lodge about midnight, at the moment when the eldest son of the deceased was making a panegyric on his beloved mother. His beautiful words, full of simple, unstudied, true eloquence, produced the liveliest sensation and emotion in all his auditory. The abundance of his tears, which did not cease to flow as long as he spoke, prevented him from continuing his long and interesting discourse. The missionary then rose, and while exhorting his good Indians to imitate the example of Louise, he expressed the sentiments of esteem and admiration which her virtues and good works had excited in his heart from his arrival in the Mission.

On the day succeeding the death of Louise, her body was carried in procession early in the morning to the church, accompanied by all the Indians of the camp. The labors of the harvest were not resumed all that day. All thought alone of giving in the most expressive manner a mark of their love, their esteem, and their grief, to the common mother of the tribe. After a solemn Mass of Requiem, and all the other funeral ceremonies of the Church, Father Gazzoli resolved to leave the body exposed during the rest of the day, to satisfy the pious zeal, we might almost say ever increasing devotion, of the many friends of the deceased. Her children, her family, all, in a word, constantly pressed around the bier, and seemed unable to tear themselves from it. It would have seemed too hard and too cruel to put an end so soon to the last expressions of affection of that religious assemblage, of those truly Christian hearts.

At last the day began to wane, and the shades of night would soon infold the valley. The missionary had to make an effort to overcome his own feelings, and to propose to his good children in Christ a separation so afflicting and so painful to their hearts. Yet it was the most favorable time to give the interment a funereal grandeur, and a last tribute of love and respect to the precious remains of Sighouin.

The funeral surpassed all expectation. The children alone, boys and girls, as a proof of their innocent love, had thought of preparing with care a large quantity of resinous splinters. These primitive torches in the hands of these children of nature, dressed chiefly in bear, wolf, jaguar, beaver, and otter skins, added to the ceremony, sad and mournful in itself, a peculiar air of wild majesty and savage grandeur, in keeping with the place and the interesting occasion of the assemblage. Perfect order was observed in the procession; modest piety and holy silence reigned in the two long files, one composed of men and the other of women, where nothing was heard but the prayer and the chant. The grave had been dug by the children and kindred of Louise. Her simple and modest coffin was the work of her youngest son. On reaching the cemetery, the Indians ranged themselves in order around the grave, and after the last funeral prayers of the Church and some words of consolation from the priest, the coffin was lowered. Each one present then threw a spadeful of earth into the grave, pronouncing a prayer and a last adieu. This touching ceremony, and the most trifling incidents of the great funeral, live in the memory of our Coeur-d'Alenes. They repeat them and will repeat them to their grandchildren; they will render ever memorable this day of Christian sorrow, this religious triumph conferred on a poor Indian woman of the Skizoumish or Coeur-d'Alenes.

In the month of February, 1859, in one of my visits to the husband of Louise, a poor old cripple, unable for many years to walk without crutches, I conversed with him on the holy life led by his wife on earth, on her noble qualities, and the great virtues of which she had given so striking an example. I asked him what he had most loved and admired in her. "Truly, Father," he replied, "I cannot tell you in what Louise most excelled. From the blessed day on which you conferred baptism upon us, all was good and admirable in her life. Never to my knowledge was there the slightest shadow of a difference between us; not a syllable, not a word louder than another. When I was sick she carried me in the canoe; if I could not use my hands, she cut my food and put it in my mouth. Louise served me like a guardian angel. Now I am an object of pity and compassion, for I am weak in mind. I love to hear her consoling words, to listen to her wise counsels, to follow her salutary advice, for she was full of the wisdom and spirit of God. The Fathers taught her many beautiful prayers, and we recited them together with our children. Now I have no one to repeat those beautiful prayers to me, and I am to be pitied. Yet I never cease thanking the Lord for the favors which he has not ceased to bestow upon me. I submit myself to his holy will; my heart is always satisfied and calm."

The good old man has always been a subject of edification amid his tribe, universally loved and respected by all the nation. He is a man of the greatest simplicity and of very solid and fervent piety; nothing gives him greater pleasure than a conversation on holy things and on the great affair of salvation. You can never visit him without seeing the smile on his lips and without finding him at prayer, with his beads in his hands. He begins to say the rosary early in the morning; the first is offered to Mary to keep him in the holy grace of the Lord during the day; he recites the others either for the missionaries, for his family, for his tribe, or for some other intention. From the day of his baptism, he made it a duty to pray for me every day, and I feel the utmost gratitude to him.

Good Adolph, such is the name of Louise's husband, related to me among other things, that during his wife's life, when the village set out for the chase, or to get wild roots, and Louise went along with them, he felt very lonesome. When he saw Louise about to die, he told her: "If you die, it will be impossible for me to stay here; I shall find the time so long, I will go back to my own land." "Take care not to do so." returned Louise; "be very careful not to do so, Adolph! Do not remove from the house of the Lord (the church). As I die here, I wish you to remain here till you die. You will not be lonesome.'' Adolph remains faithful to his wife's recommendation. His cabin is beside the church, and although alone the greater part of the time since the death of Louise, he has not felt the time tedious for a single moment. His beads and prayer are his greatest consolation, and his only delight.

On my recent visit to the Coeur-d'Alenes, I again questioned the Indians, in order to obtain new details as to the life of Louise Sighouin. The answer was this: ''After so many years it is difficult to add any thing to these extraordinary facts, so well known by all, except that from the time of her baptism, her life was an act of continual charity.'' And I can say, and all that read this narrative will agree with me, that there is no exaggeration in this summary remark. It was a devotedness of every day and every hour, a chain of links of little details of mercy, which offer nothing very striking, unless it be that untiring constancy, which for more than ten years, was always prompt night and day in exercising all works of charity, corporal and spiritual. No one will better appreciate this martyrdom of detail than those who are themselves devoted to it; and if we consider that Louise was poor, infirm, that she could only half understand the missionaries, who as yet only stammered the language of the Indians, no one will call in doubt the many graces which Louise received, and the immense profit she derived from the lessons of her Divine Master. God had raised up Louise to be the assistant of the apostolic men in the outset of their labors, when they did not understand the language. It had been the same at the mission of St. Ignatius. The Almighty had given the missionaries the chief Loyola to do among the Kalispels what Louise has done among the Coeur-d'Alenes. Both were poor and infirm; it was a lively faith which animated their zeal; both devoted themselves to their last sigh, and both were bitterly deplored after their death. Loyola displayed invincible firmness. ''As long as I have a breath of life, my people must walk uprightly,'' said he; and his virtue alone gave him the authority to speak so. Louise on the contrary had no support in her zeal except her admirable meekness, her unwearied patience. Both died about the same time, when the missionaries began to be generally understood by the Indians.

I have all these circumstances from the missionaries on the spot, especially from the reverend and worthy Father Gazzoli, nephew of the cardinal of that name who died in 1858. This Father is at this moment Superior of the Mission of the Sacred Heart among the Skizoumish or Coeur-d'Alenes.

In one of my letters written ten years ago, June 4, 1849, I said: ''This extraordinary attention of the Indians, and this avidity on their part for the word of God, must seem surprising in a people who appear to combine all moral and intellectual miseries. But the spirit of the Lord breathes where it pleases him, his graces and his light prompt and aid men whom ignorance, rather than a perverse or disorderly will, has rendered evil. And that same spirit which obliged the most rebellious to cry out with St. Paul: 'Lord! what wilt thou have me to do?' can often soften the fiercest hearts, inflame the coldest, produce peace, justice, and joy, where iniquity, trouble, and disorder reigned. The great respect and attention which the poor Indians show on all occasions to the missionary who comes to announce to them the word of God, are a source of great consolation and encouragement. He finds the finger of God in the spontaneous manifestations of these unhappy men.'' Since the Gospel has been announced to the tribes of the Rocky Mountains, the Lord has always had his chosen souls among them. In the different missions, many neophytes are distinguished by a zeal and piety truly worthy of the primitive Christians, by a rare assiduity at all religious exercises, by the faithful accomplishment of all the duties of a good Christian, in a word, by all the virtues which we have just seen in their highest form in Louise Sighouin.

INDIAN SKETCHES.

LETTER OF FATHER JOSET TO FATHER FOUILLOT

SACRED HEART MISSION, 21st June, 1859.

I HAVE just received your kind letter of March 12th, 1858; it was more than a year on the way. I hasten to comply with your request by saying a word as to our labors. The language is the greatest difficulty. One must learn it as best he can. There is no written language, there are no interpreters, there is very little analogy with other tongues. The pronunciation is very harsh, the turn of thought is entirely different from ours. They have no abstract ideas, every thing is concrete. And with these elements it is necessary to create a religious, and even spiritual, phraseology: for the savages know nothing that is not material.

I have been here nearly fifteen years. I am not yet master of the language, and am far from flattering myself with the hope of becoming so. My catechist remarked to me the other day, "You pronounce like a child learning to talk, when you speak of religion, we understand you well; but when you change the subject, it is another thing.'' That is all I want. I have at last succeeded in translating the catechism. I think it is nearly correct. You can hardly imagine what it cost me to do it. I have been constantly at work at it since my arrival here. I finished it only last winter. Nevertheless, it is very short; it has but fourteen lessons. It is based upon the first part of the Catechism of Lyons, which was in use in the diocese of St. Louis (of which this mission formed a part) upon our arrival. This catechism is printed, not on paper, but on the memory of the children: they know it all by heart, questions and answers, and they say two lessons of it every day after morning prayer; so that they say the whole of it once a week. The good will of these poor Indians is admirable; I never saw or heard of any thing to equal it. I am never tired of hearing them their catechism; on the contrary, it is my greatest pleasure. Oh, if you could have seen what passed here last winter, how your Reverence would love these poor savages, and how you would pray the Queen of Apostles to send them missionaries. Thirty children made their first communion together, and I cannot even yet think of the manner in which they prepared for it, without emotion.

From the end of November to Palm Sunday, on which day this ceremony took place, they had catechism at the church three times a day, and it was rare that one missed the exercise: besides this there was a repetition, every day, either before the chief or the catechist. Every time that I gave them permission to assemble in my apartment for more ample explanations, they crowded there, remaining in postures of the greatest discomfort for three-quarters of an hour or an hour at a time, without ceasing to give me the utmost attention. They never became weary. There was no end to private recitations among themselves, and little bands would everywhere be found retired and reciting the catechism. When visiting the sick in the evening, I was almost certain to hear, in some tent, or other, groups of children reciting catechism, the more advanced helping the others; and this zeal for instruction increased rather than diminished.

During the month of January, the period of the great deer hunt, the children came to ask my permission to return to their parents: this period is that of harvest with them. How could I refuse them. They were actually suffering with hunger at the Mission; besides, their parents themselves had expressed the desire to see them. "How much holiday do you want?" "Four weeks." "I allow it." It was not too much. I see nothing very surprising in the fact that a boy, after a vacation of two months, may be glad to return to school. Solitude and inaction have become wearisome to him. But the case with my dusky children of the forest is very different. At camp there is no want of occupation or of companions, they have food in abundance, which is rarely the case at the Mission. This year, in particular, the scarcity has been great. Nevertheless, they obtained of their parents the permission to shorten their vacation by one half. With their snow-shoes on their feet, and their bundles on their backs, they made a distance of ten leagues (28 miles English), crossing a mountain covered with a thick forest, over soft snow. You must be on the spot to know what are the fatigues of such a journey. Judge of my surprise when I saw them all enter my room at nightfall, worn out with fatigue, but gay and happy. What motive could induce them to leave the abundance they were enjoying with their parents, to come to the privations of the Mission? I know of no other than their desire to be instructed in order to make their first Communion. They knew well enough that I had nothing to give them but the bread of the Divine Word. For, be it said, by the way, although I give catechism three hundred times a year, I doubt whether there is a catechist in the world more utterly deprived of the means of encouraging his pupils. Some prayer-beads would have been a great reward, but I could give them nothing but a medal to each as a memorial of their first Communion. I was almost tempted to regret my poverty. In Europe there are many pious souls to encourage poor children in like circumstances but here, on the borders of the world, want has no witness but the missionary, who can give it only his sighs. The mines have ruined us, and it is precisely when prices have doubled, that our resources have diminished, so that instead of giving catechism, one is often obliged to rack one's brains to make both ends meet. All that I have said of my dear children is the exact truth, without exaggeration. I am no poet. However, I begin to fear that I shall be reminded of the fable of the owl and the eagle; so, though I have much yet to tell, I will stop here.

However I cannot but beg you, and those to whom you may communicate these lines, to recommend these dear children to our Lady of Fourvieres, that she may obtain for them the gift of perseverance. They are exposed to many dangers. Not to speak of others, strong liquors have already found their way into the neighboring tribes: and I know that the wretches who make it their business thus to ruin the poor savages, boast that our people will not be able to resist the temptation more than the others. If their infernal predictions should be realized, you may see me again one day in Europe.

I do not know to whom to address myself to convey our thanks to the Ladies of the Sacred Heart. We received, some years since, two sets of very fine vestments, for our Church of the Sacred Heart, from some unknown benefactors. I have just learned that the present was from those ladies, but I know not of what House. By the way, no one sees our church without testifying his astonishment. It is entirely the work of the Indians, except the altars. It is a magnificent monument to the faith of the Coeur-d'Alenes, who have given the lie to their name by its erection. If it were finished, it would be a handsome church even in Europe. The design is by Father Ravalli. It is 90 feet long by 40 wide. It has 29 pillars, 2½ feet square by 25 feet in height. All the rest is of timber, and in proportion. It was all cut, raised, and roofed by the savages, under the direction of a Father; they also filled it in, and built the foundation-walls, which are from two to five feet high, and of proportionate thickness. The Indians brought the stones from a distance of eight hundred feet, did all the mason work, and would accept no recompense. It is a great grief to us that we cannot finish it. There are two fine altars, with handsome pictures of the Sacred Heart and of the Blessed Virgin, but all the rest is naked, without doors, windows, or flooring, and not being framed in on the outside, I fear it will rot before it is completed. The neophytes have done their best: but in the absence of resources, we cannot continue the work.

Mission of St. Ignatius at Kalispell Bay Among the Pend d'Oreilles

LETTER OF FATHER DE SMET

ST. LOUIS, NOV. 1, 1859.

REVEREND AND DEAR FATHER:

IN accordance with your request, I proceed with great pleasure to give you some details of my recent journey.

On the 20th of May, 1858, I set out from St. Louis for the western portion of North America, and after an absence of about sixteen months, I returned to the point from whence I set out. During this interval, I had accompanied, as chaplain, an army sent out by the United States against the Mormons and the savages. I propose to give you some details of this double expedition. Not to fatigue you, I will endeavor to be brief. At best, however, my narrative will fill some pages, as my recent voyage has been very long. It exceeded fifteen thousand English miles, or five thousand leagues. I propose then to give you some details in regard to the different countries I have traversed, and the seas I have crossed, and of my visit to the savage tribes, my dear spiritual children of the Rocky Mountains, the Coeur-d'Alenes, Kalispels, Pends-d'Oreilles, Flatheads, and Kootenays; of my stay among the different tribes of the Great Plains of the Upper Missouri, and of the manner in which my time was spent in the army of the United States in quality of chaplain, and envoy extraordinary of that Government. These details, I venture to hope, will not be without interest for you, and they will form the subject of my little sketch.

Several years have passed, since the Mormons, that terrible sect of modern fanatics, flying from civilization, settled in the midst of an uninhabited wilderness. With hearts full of hate and bitterness, they never ceased on every occasion which presented itself, to agitate the country, provoke the inhabitants, and commit acts of robbery and murder against many travellers and adventurers from the United States. In September, 1857, one hundred and twenty emigrants from Arkansas, men, women, and children, are said to have been horribly massacred by the Mormons, in a place called the Mountain Meadows. These fanatics never ceased to defy the government, and announced that the day had arrived to avenge the death of their prophet, Joseph and his brother, and to retaliate the wrongs and acts of injustice and cruelty of which they pretended to have been the victims in the States of Missouri and Illinois, whence they had been forcibly expelled by the inhabitants.

On two different occasions, the governor and subaltern officers, sent by the President of the United States, had met with such strong opposition from the Mormons in the attempt to accomplish their respective duties, that they were forced to quit the Territory of Utah, and to return to lay their complaints before the President. Congress resolved to send a third governor, accompanied, this time, by two thousand soldiers, who were to be followed by from two to four thousand others in the following spring of 1858. I accompanied the last named expedition. On the 15th of May, 1858, the Minister of War wrote to me as follows:—

"The President is desirous to engage you to attend the army for Utah, to officiate as chaplain. In his opinion your services would be important in many respects to the public interest, particularly in the present condition of our affairs in Utah. Having sought information as to the proper person to be thus employed his attention has been directed to you, and he has instructed me to address you on the subject, in the hope that you may consider it not incompatible with your clerical duties or your personal feelings to yield to his request,'' &c.

The Reverend Father Provincial and all the other consultors, considering the circumstances, expressed themselves in favor of my accepting. I immediately set out for Fort Leavenworth, Kansas Territory, to join the army at that point. On the very day of my arrival, I took my place in the Seventh Regiment, composed of eight hundred men under the command of the excellent Colonel Morrison, whose staff was composed of a numerous body of superior officers of the line and engineers. General Harney, the commander-in-chief, and one of the most distinguished and most valiant generals of the United States, with great courtesy, installed me himself in my post. The brave colonel, though a Protestant, thanked him very heartily. ''General,'' said he, ''I thought myself highly honored when intrusted with the command of the engineers: to have attached to my command a representative of the ancient and venerable Church, I hold as an additional favor.'' General Harney then shook hands with me, with great kindness, bade me welcome to the army, and assured me that I should be left perfectly free in the exercise of my holy ministry among the soldiers. He kept his word most loyally, and in this he was seconded by all the officers. During the whole time that I was among them, I never met with the slightest obstacle in the discharge of my duties. The soldiers had always free access to my tent for confession and instruction. I had frequently the consolation of celebrating the holy sacrifice of the Mass early in the morning, and on each occasion, a large number of soldiers devoutly approached the holy table.

A word or two in regard to the character of the countries through which we passed, will perhaps be agreeable to you. I left Fort Leavenworth on the 1st of June, 1858, in the Seventh Regiment, commanded by the worthy Colonel Morrison. I had an opportunity of observing with admiration the extraordinary rapidity of the progress of civilization in Kansas. A space of 276 miles was already in great part occupied by white settlers. No further back than 1851, at the time of my return from the great council, held on the borders of the Platte or Nebraska river, the plains of Kansas were almost entirely without inhabitants, containing only a few scattered villages of Indians, living for the most part by the chase, by fishing, and on wild fruit and roots. But eight years have made an entire change: many towns and villages have sprung up, as it were, by enchantment; forges and mills of every kind are already very numerous; extensive and beautiful farms have been established in all directions with extraordinary rapidity and industry. The face of the country is entirely changed. In 1851, the antelope, the wild deer, and the wild goat, bounded at liberty over these extensive plains, nor is it much longer ago that these fields were the pasture of enormous herds of buffaloes; to-day they are in the possession of numerous droves of horned cattle, sheep and hogs, horses and mules. The fertile soil rewards a hundredfold the labors of the husbandman. Wheat, corn, barley, oats, flax, hemp, all sorts of garden stuff and all the fruits of the temperate zone, are produced there in abundance. Emigration tends thither, and commerce follows in its tracks and acquires new importance every day.

Leavenworth is the principal town of Kansas Territory. It contains already about ten thousand souls, though it has sprung into existence within the last six years. It is beautifully and advantageously situated on the Missouri river. It has a bishop, two Catholic churches, a convent with a boarding-school and a day-school. There are already fifteen churches, twenty-three stations, sixteen priests, five religious communities, and four manual-labor schools for the Osage and Potawatomie Indians, which are under the care of our Fathers and Religious Ladies of different orders.

The greater portion of the Territory is not thickly wooded:

the surface of the country, as a general thing, is rolling and well adapted to agriculture; it is not unlike the billows of a vast ocean, suddenly arrested in its flow and converted into solid land. The air is fresh and wholesome. As one rises with the elevations of the soil, the graceful undulation of the alternating vale and hill contrast admirably with the waving lines of walnut trees, oaks, and poplars, which mark the course of each little river. The banks of each stream are generally more or less thickly wooded. We ascended the valley of the Little Blue for three days, making a distance of fifty-three miles. The names of the principal plants which attract the attention of the botanist in the plains of Kansas, are: the *anothera,* with its brilliant yellow flowers, the *amorpha* and *artemisia,* the *commelina,* the blue and purple *lupin,* different forms and species of *cactus,* the *pradescantia,* the *mimosa,* and the white *mimulus.* The waters of the Little Blue are left at a distance of 275 miles from Fort Leavenworth. Continuing the route from that point, you cross elevated prairies of a distance of twenty-six miles, and enter the great valley of the Nebraska or Platte river, at the distance of fifteen miles from Fort Kearney. This river, up to its two forks, is about three thousand yards wide; its waters are yellowish and muddy in the spring freshets, and resemble those of the Missouri and the Mississippi; it is not so deep as those streams; its current is very rapid. Fort Kearney is rather insignificant. It consists of three or four frame houses and several made of *adobes,* a kind of coarse brick baked in the sun. The Government has a military post there for the tranquillity of the country, and to provide for the safety of travellers crossing the desert to go to California, Oregon, and the Territories of Utah and Washington.

A great number of Pawnee Indians were encamped at a little distance from the Fort. I came near witnessing a battle between them and a war party of Arapahoes, who, favored by the night, had succeeded in approaching the camp unseen almost forty strong. The Pawnees had just let their horses loose at break of day, when the enemy, with loud cries, rushed into the drove, and carried away many hundreds with them at full gallop. The alarm immediately spread throughout the camp. The Pawnees, indifferently armed and almost naked, rushed in pursuit of the Arapahoes, caught up with them, and a combat more noisy than bloody took place. A young Pawnee chief, the most impetuous of his band, was killed and three of his companions wounded. The Arapahoes lost one killed and many wounded. Desirous to stop the combat, I hurried to the scene of battle with an aid-de-camp of the general, but all was over when we arrived; The Pawnees were returning with their dead and wounded and all the stolen horses. On their return to camp, nothing was heard but cries of sorrow, rage, and despair, with threats and vociferations against their enemies. It was a harrowing scene. The deceased warrior was decorated and painted with all the marks of distinction of a great brave, and loaded with his finest ornaments. They placed him in the grave amid the acclamations and lamentations of the whole tribe.

The next day the Pawnee-Loups invited me to their camp. I found there two French Creoles, old acquaintances of mine, of the Rocky Mountains. They received me with the greatest kindness, and desired to act as my interpreters. I had a long conference on religion with these poor, unhappy savages. They listened with the most earnest attention. After the instruction they presented to me 208 little children, and very earnestly begged me to regenerate them in the holy waters of baptism. These savages have been the terror of travellers obliged to pass through their territory; for many years their character has been that of thieves, drunkards, and ruffians, and they are brutalized by drink, which they readily obtain, owing to their proximity to the frontiers of civilization. This accursed traffic has always and everywhere been the ruin of the Indian tribes, and it leads to their rapid extinction.

Two days' march above Fort Kearney, at a place called Cottonwood Springs, I found thirty lodges of Ogallallas, a Sioux or Dacotah tribe. At their request I baptized all their children. In 1851, at the Great Council on the Platte, I had brought them the same blessing. They told me that a great number of their children had died since, carried off by epidemics, which had raged among the nomadic tribes of the plains. They are much consoled at the thought of the happiness which children obtain by holy baptism. They know its high importance, and appreciate it as the greatest favor which they can receive.

General Harney had many friendly conferences with the Pawnees, the Ogallallas, and the Sheyennes in which he strongly advised them to cease molesting the whites who might pass through their borders, adding that on this condition alone could they remain at peace with the United States.

I have so often spoken of the buffalo in my letters, that this time I might pass him by in silence. However, I will mention it for the purpose of saying that the race is not extinct in these parts, though it is becoming more rare to find buffaloes on the highway across the plains, which its instinct must have taught it to avoid. We met our first herds of this noble animal in the neighborhood of Fort Kearney. The sight created great excitement among those soldiers who had not visited the plains before, and they burned to bring down one or two. Armed, as they were, with the famous Minie rifles, they might have made a good hunt, had they not been on foot, while the buffaloes were at full gallop; it was, therefore, impossible to get near them. They fired, however, at a distance of two hundred or three hundred yards. A single buffalo was wounded in the leg. Its wound compelled it to lag behind, and he became the target of all our men. A confused sound of cries and rifle shots arose, as if the last hour had come for the last buffalo. Riddled with balls, his tongue lolling out, the blood streaming from his throat and nostrils, the brute fell at last. To cut him up and distribute the meat was the work of a moment. Never was buffalo more rapidly transformed into steak and soup,—every one would have his piece.

While these things were going on, Captain P______, mounted on a fine horse, approached a bull, already terrified by the rifle shots and the terrible noise of our soldiers, who were novices to the chase, and fired at him twice almost point blank. The buffalo and the horse stopped at the same instant. In spite of all his efforts, Captain P______ could not make his horse, unaccustomed to the hunt, advance a single step, and the furious buffalo plunged both horns into his flank and threw him down dead. In this critical moment the courageous rider did not lose his presence of mind: he leaped from his horse over the buffalo's back, gave him two more bullets from his six-shooter, and completely baffled him. The captain then fled to a gully, which was luckily both deep and near at hand. The buffalo, unable to follow him, abandoned his persecutor, who returned to camp with his horse's saddle on his back. A horse must be well trained to hunt the buffalo, and must be trained specially for buffalo hunting: otherwise the danger is very great, and the consequence may be fatal.

During the months of June and July, tempests and falls of rain and hail are very frequent, and almost of daily occurrence, towards evening in the valley of the Platte, which is the country of storms and whirlwinds *par excellence*. The gathering of these storms can be noticed at a great distance, as at sea. At first, light spots of clouds are observed on the horizon, which are followed by dark masses of cloud, which move along in succession, crowding one upon another, and spreading over the sky with extraordinary rapidity, they approach and cross each other; they burst and pour forth torrents of water, which drench the valleys, or volleys of hail which crush the herbs and flowers: the storm-clouds then disappear as rapidly as they have come. "Every evil has its remedy," says the old proverb, and these hurricanes, storms, and heavy rains, serve the purpose of cooling and purifying the atmosphere, which at this season would become insupportable but for this circumstance. The mercury often rises to one hundred degrees of Fahrenheit in the shade. The water does not rest long on the surface of the soil: it is absorbed almost as it falls on account of the very porous character of the earth of the valley and its sandy bottom. Travellers, in camps a little removed from the river, always dig wells; the water is everywhere found at a depth of two or three feet. This water, though cold and clear, must be unwholesome, and frequently causes severe sickness. Graves abound in these regions, and the mortal remains of a vast number of emigrants repose there. With these emigrants have also sunk beneath the valley of the Platte that ardent thirst for gold, those desires and ambitious projects for wealth, greatness, and pleasure, which devoured them, and drove them towards the distant regions of California, Pike's Peak, and Fraser. Death met them far from their Penates, and they are buried in these desert strands. How uncertain are the affairs of this world! Man makes his plans; he builds his castles in the air; he counts upon a future which does not belong to him: he proposes, but God disposes, and cuts the thread of life in the midst of these vain hopes.

The most remarkable thing that I met on this occasion on the highway of the prairies, ordinarily so lonely, were the long wagon trains engaged in transporting to Utah provisions and stores of war. If the journals of the day may be believed, these cost the Government fifteen millions. Each train consisted of twenty-six wagons, each wagon drawn by six yoke of oxen, and containing near five thousand pounds. The Quarter-master-general made the calculation, and told me that the whole train would make a line of about fifty miles. We passed every day some wagons of this immense train. Each wagon marked with a name as in the case of ships, and these names served to furnish amusement to the passer-by; the caprices of the captains in this respect having imposed upon the wagons such names as the *Constitution,* the *President,* the *Great Republic,* the *King of Bavaria, Lola Montes, Louis Napoleon, Dan. O'Connell, Old Kentuck, &c., &c.* These were daubed in great letters on each side of the carriage. On the plains, the wagoner assumes the style of *captain*, being placed in command of his wagon and twelve oxen. The master-wagoner is admiral of this little land-fleet: he has control of 26 captains and 312 oxen. At a distance, the white awnings of the wagons have the effect of a fleet of vessels with all canvas spread.

On leaving Leavenworth the drivers look well enough, being all in new clothes, but as they advance into the plains, their good clothes become travel-stained and torn, and at last are converted into rags. The *captains* have hardly proceeded two hundred miles, before their trail is marked with rags, scattered and flying along the route. You may often remark also on the various camping grounds, even as far as the Rocky Mountains, and beyond, the wrecks of wagons and the skeletons of oxen, but especially the remains of the wardrobe of the traveller: legs of pantaloons and drawers, a shirt-bosom, the back or the arm of a flannel vest, stockings out at toe and heel, crownless hats, and shoes worn through in the soles or uppers, are strewed along the route. These deserted camps are also marked by packs of cards strewed round among broken jars and bottles; here you see a gridiron, a coffee-pot, or a tin bowl; there a cooking-stove and the fragments of a shaving-dish, all worn out and cast aside. The poor Indians regard these signs of encroaching civilization with an unquiet eye as they pass them on their way. These rags and refuse are to them the harbingers of the approach of a dismal future for themselves; they announce to them that the plains and forest over which they roam in the chase, their beautiful lakes and rivers swarming with fish, and the repair of numerous aquatic birds; the hearth which witnessed their birth, and the soil which covers the ashes of their fathers,—all, in fine, that is most dear to them,—are about to pass into the hands of the rapacious white man: and they, poor mortals, accustomed to roam at large, and over a vast space, free like the birds of the air, will be inclosed in narrow reserves, far from their cherished hunting grounds and fine fisheries, far from their fields of roots and fruits; or driven back into the mountains or to unknown shores. It is not surprising, then, that the savage seeks sometimes to revenge himself on the white man; it is rarely, however, that he is the aggressor: surely, not once out of ten provoking cases.

The wagons are formed every evening into a *corral*. That is, the whole twenty-six are ranged in a circle, and chained one to the other, so as to leave only one opening, to give passage to the beasts, which pass the night in the centre, and are guarded there by several sentinels under arms. Under the protection of a small number of determined men, the wagons and animals are secure from any attack of undisciplined Indians, in however great numbers. When the travellers neglect this precaution, and camp at random, not unfrequently a hostile band of Indians will provoke what is called a *stampede*, or panic among the cattle, and carry them all off at once. The travellers go into camp early, and at break of day the beasts are let loose in the prairie that they may have plenty of time to graze. Grass is very abundant in the valley of the Platte, and on the neighboring acclivities.

Between Fort Kearney and the crossing of the South Fork of the Platte, we met over a hundred families of Mormons on their way to Kansas and Missouri, with the intention of settling there. They appeared delighted at being fortunate enough to leave, safe and sound, the famous promised land of Utah; thanks to the influence of the new governor, and the presence of the United States troops. They told us that a great number of other families would follow them, so soon as they should be capable of doing so, and of procuring the necessary means for the journey. They confessed that they would have escaped long before, had they not been afraid of falling into the hands of the Danites, or Destroying Angels. These compose the body-guard of the Prophet; they are said to be entirely and blindly at his disposal, to carry out all his plans, meet all his wishes, and execute all his measures, which often involve robbery and murder. Before the arrival of the United States soldiers, woe to any one who manifested a desire to leave Utah, or abandon the sect: woe to him who dared to raise a voice against the actions of the Prophet,—they rarely escaped the poniards of these Destroying Angels, or rather incarnate demons.

The highway of the plains, during the beautiful season of 1858, appeared, as it were, invaded by an unusual and joyous animation. To complete the idea which I have just given, I will add that couriers and express messengers, coming and returning, constantly crossed each other on the road. The different companies of the army left a space of two or three days' journey between them. Each company was followed by ambulances for the use of the superior officers, a body of artillery and engineers, and a train of wagons, with six mules each, transporting provisions and baggage. Each company was followed also by an immense drove of six or seven hundred horned cattle, to furnish their daily food. Uncle Sam, as the Government of the United States is called, has a truly paternal heart; he provides abundantly for the wants of the defenders of the country, and will not suffer them to want their comforts.

Every thing was going on admirably and in good order. The commanding general and staff were already at the crossing of the south branch of the Platte, 480 miles from Fort Leavenworth, when he received the news that the Mormons had submitted, and laid down their arms, and at the same time an order to distribute his troops to other points, and return to the United States. This also changed my destination; the conclusion of peace put an end to my little diplomatic mission to the Indian tribes of Utah. I consulted with the general, and accompanied him on his return to Leavenworth.

The South Fork of the Platte, at the crossing, is 2045 feet wide. In the month of July, its depth is generally about three feet, after the junction of the two forks, the width is about 3000 yards. The bottom, throughout the whole length, is sandy.

I could say much, dear Father, about the country between Leavenworth and the South Pass of the Platte, its botanical and other properties and productions, but I have spoken of these on many occasions in my letters describing other journeys across this region. The little incidents mentioned in this letter are all connected with my last trip.

Before leaving Fort Leavenworth for St. Louis, I made a little excursion of seventy miles to visit our dear Fathers and Brothers of the Mission of St. Mary among the Pottawatomies. I at last reached St. Louis in the beginning of September, after a first absence of about three months, and after a journey, to and fro, of 1976 miles. My stay in St. Louis was short. I will, in my next letter, give you details, which will inform you as to the particulars of the long expedition of which I speak in the first part of this letter.

Receive, Reverend and Dear Father, the expression of those sentiments of respect and affection which you know I entertain for you, and let me recommend myself very specially to your holy sacrifices and good prayers,

your Reverence's servant in Christ,

P.J. DE SMET, S.J.

The Peace Delegation of 1859. Seated in the front row are the chiefs: Kalispel Victor; Pend d'Oreille Alexander; Flathead Adolphus; Coeur d'Alene Andrew Seltice. Standing in the back row left to right are: Chaudiere Denis; Coeur d'Alene Bonaventure; Father De Smet; and Iroquois Francis Saxa.

LETTER OF FATHER DE SMET.

ST. LOUIS, NOV. 10, 1859.

REVEREND AND DEAR FATHER:

IN ACCORDANCE with my promise, I resume the little story of my long voyage. On my return to St. Louis, I tendered to the Minister of War my resignation of the post of chaplain. It was not accepted, because a new war had just broken out against the Government, among the tribes of the Rocky Mountains. I was notified by telegraph to proceed to New York, and to embark there with General Harney and his staff.

On the 20th of September, 1858, we left the port of New York for Aspinwall; it was the season of the equinox, so that we experienced some rough weather in the voyage, and a heavy wind among the Bahamas. We coasted for some time along the eastern shore of Cuba, in sight of the promontories of St. Domingo and Jamaica. On the 29th I crossed the Isthmus of Panama on a good railroad, forty-seven miles long. The next day I had the happiness to offer the holy sacrifice of the Mass in the cathedral of Panama. The bishop very earnestly entreated me to use my influence with the Very Reverend Father General at Rome, to obtain for him a colony of Jesuits. His lordship especially expressed his earnest desire to intrust his ecclesiastical seminary to the care of the Society of Jesus. New Granada, as well as many other regions of Spanish

South America, offers, doubtless, a vast field to the zeal of a large number of our Fathers.

The distance from Panama to San Francisco is more than three thousand miles. The steamer brought to in the superb bay of Acapulco to receive the mails, and to coal and water: this is a little port of Mexico. On the evening of the 16th of October, I arrived at San Francisco, happy to find myself in a house of the Society, and in the company of many of my brethren in Jesus Christ, who loaded me with kindness, and all the attention of the most cordial charity. The *"quam bonum et jucundum habitare fratres in unum"* is especially appreciated, when one leaves a California steamer in which one has been imprisoned, sometimes with fourteen or fifteen hundred individuals, all laboring under the gold fever, and who think and speak of nothing but mines of gold, and all the terrestrial delights which this gold is shortly to procure them. However, the "shortly" is long enough to allow of the destruction or disappearance of many an illusion. "All that glitters is not gold."

We left San Francisco on the 20th, and in a few days made more than one thousand miles to Fort Vancouver, on the Columbia river. The news of the cessation of hostilities, and of the submission of the tribes, had been received at Vancouver. The task remained of removing the Indian prejudices, soothing their inquietude and alarm, and correcting, or rather refuting, the false rumors which are generally spread after a war, and which, otherwise, might be the cause of its renewal.

Under the orders of the general commanding in chief, I left Fort Vancouver on the 29th of October, to go among the tribes of the mountains, at a distance of about eight hundred miles. I visited the Catholic soldiers of Fort Dalles City and Walla-walla on my way. At the last-named fort, I had the consolation of meeting Reverend F. Congiato, on his return from his visit to the Missions, and of receiving very cheering news from him as to the disposition of the Indians. At my request, the excellent commandant of the fort had the very great kindness to set at liberty all the prisoners and hostages, both Coeur-d'Alenes and Spokans, and he intrusted to my charge to bring them on their way, and return them to their respective nations. These good Indians, particularly the Coeur d'Alenes, had given the greatest edification to the soldiers during their captivity: these men often approached them with admiration, in witnessing the performance of their pious exercises, morning and evening, and in listening to their prayers and hymns. During the whole journey, these good Indians testified the utmost gratitude to me, and their punctual performance of their religious duties was a source of great consolation and happiness to me.

On the 21st of November I arrived at the Mission of the Sacred Heart, among the Coeur-d'Alenes. I was detained at the Mission by the snow until the 18th of February, 1859. During this interval snow fell with more or less abundance for forty-three days and nights, on seven days it rained, we had twenty-one cloudy days, and sixteen days of clear and cold weather. I left the Mission on the 18th of February with the Reverend Father Joset, who accompanied me until we met Father Hoecken, who had promised to meet us on Clarke's River. The ice, snow, rain, and winds, impeded very much our course, in our frail canoes of bark, on the rivers and great lakes: we often ran considerable risk in crossing rapids and falls, of which Clarke's River is full. I counted thirty-four of these in seventy miles. We met with several camps of Indians in winter-quarters on every side. On the approach of the winter season, they are obliged to scatter in the forests and along the lakes and rivers, where they live by the chase and fishing. They received us everywhere with the greatest kindness, and, notwithstanding their extreme poverty, willingly shared with us their small rations and meagre provisions. They eagerly embraced the occasion to attend to their religious duties and other exercises of piety: attending at the instructions with great attention, and with much zeal and fervor, at Mass, and at morning and evening prayers. On the 11th of March we arrived at the Mission of St. Ignatius, among the Pends-d'Oreilles of the mountains.

The Kootenays, a neighboring tribe to the Pends-d'Oreilles, having heard of my arrival, had travelled many days' journey through the snow to shake hands with me, to bid me welcome, and manifest their filial affection. In 1845 I had made some stay with them. I was the first priest who had announced to them the glad tidings of salvation and I had baptized all their little children and large number of adults. They came on this occasion, with a primitive simplicity, to assure me that they had remained faithful to prayer, that is, to religion, and all the good advice that they had received. All the Fathers spoke to me of these good Kootenays in the highest terms. Fraternal union, evangelic simplicity, innocence, and peace, still reign among them in full vigor. Their honesty is so great and so well known, that the trader leaves his store-house entirely, the door remaining unlocked often during his absence for weeks. The Indians go in and out, and help themselves to what they need, and settle with the trader on his return. He assured me himself, that in doing business with them in this style he never lost the value of a pin.

On the 18th of March I crossed deep snow a distance of seventy miles, to St. Mary's valley, to revisit my first and ancient spiritual children of the mountains, the poor and abandoned Flatheads. They were greatly consoled on learning that Very Rev. Father General had the intention of causing the mission to be undertaken again. The principal chiefs assured me that since the departure of the Fathers, they had continued to assemble morning and evenings for prayers, to ring the angelus at the accustomed hour, and to rest on Sunday, to glorify the holy day of our Lord. I will not enter into long details here, as to the present dispositions of this little tribe, for fear of being too long. Doubtless, in the absence of the missionaries, the enemy of souls has committed some ravages among them, but by the grace of God the evil is not irreparable.

Their daily practices of piety, and the conferences I held with them during several days, have given me the consoling conviction that the faith is still maintained among the Flatheads, and still brings forth fruits of salvation among them,—their greatest chieftains, Michael, Adolphe, Ambrose, Moses, and others, are true and zealous Christians, and real piety in religion and true valor at war are united in them.

In my several visits to the stations in the Rocky Mountains, I was received by the Indians with every demonstration of sincere and filial joy. I think I may say that my presence among them has been of some advantage to them, both in a religious and secular point of view. I did my best to encourage them to persevere in piety, and to maintain the conditions of the treaty of peace with the Government. In these visits I had the happiness to baptize over a hundred infants, and a large number of adults.

On the 16th of April, in accordance with the orders of the commander-in-chief of the army, I went to Fort Vancouver, and left the Mission of St. Ignatius. At my request, all the chiefs of the different mountain tribes accompanied me, to renew the treaty of peace with the general and with the Superintendent of Indian Affairs; I give their names, and the nations to which they belonged. Alexander *Temglagketzin,* or the Man-without-a-horse, great chief of the Pends-d'Oreilles: Victor *Alamiken,* or the Happy-man (he deserves his name, for he is a saintly man), great chief of the Kalispels; Adolphus *Kwilkweschape,* or Red-feather, chief of the Flatheads; Francis *Saxa*, or the Iroquois, another Flathead chief; Dennis *Zenemtietze,* or the Thunders-robe, chief of the Schuyelpi or Chaudieres; Andrew and Bonaventure, chiefs and braves among the Coeur-d'Alenes, or Skizoumish; *Kamiakin,* great chief of the Yacomans; and Gerry great chief of the Spokans. The last two are still pagans, though their children have been baptized. We suffered much, and ran many dangers on the route, on account of the high stage of the rivers and the heavy snow. For three days we had to clear a way through thick forests, where thousands of trees, thrown down by storms, lay across one another, and were covered. four, six, and eight feet, with snow; several horses perished in this dangerous passage. My horse stumbled many a time, and procured me many a fall; but aside from some serious bruises and scratches, a hat battered to pieces, a torn pair of trowsers, and a *soutane* or black-gown in rags, I came out of it safe and sound. I measured white cedars in the wood, which were as much as six or seven persons could clasp at the base, and of proportionate height. After a month's journey, we arrived at Fort Vancouver.

On the 18th of May the interview took place with the general, the superintendent, and the Indian chiefs. It produced most happy results on both sides. About three weeks' time was accorded to the chiefs to visit, at the cost of Government, the principal cities and towns of the State of Oregon and Washington Territory, with every thing remarkable in the way of industrial establishments, steam-engines, forges, manufactories, and printing establishments,—of all which the poor Indians can make nothing or very little. The visit which appeared the most to interest the chiefs, was that which they made to the prison at Portland, and its wretched inmates, whom they found chained within its cells. They were particularly interested in the causes, motives, and duration of their imprisonment. Chief Alexander kept it in his mind. Immediately on his return to his camp at St. Ignatius Mission he assembled his people, and related to them all the wonders of the whites, and especially the history of the prison. "We," said he, "have neither chains nor prisons; and for want of them, no doubt, a great number of us are wicked and have deaf ears. As chief, I am determined to do my duty: I shall take a whip to punish the wicked; let all those who have been guilty of any misdemeanor present themselves, I am ready." The known guilty parties were called upon by name, many presented themselves of their own accord, and all received a proportionate correction.

Before leaving the parts of civilization, all the chiefs received presents from the general and superintendent, and returned to their own country contented and happy, and well determined to keep at peace with the whites. As for me, I had accomplished among the Indians the task which the Government had imposed upon me. I explained to the general my motives for desiring to return to St. Louis by way of the interior. He acceded to my desire with the greatest affability, and in an answer which he addressed to me on this matter, he bore most honorable testimony to my services.

About the 15th of June, I again left Vancouver with the chiefs, to return to the mountains. I passed the 7th, 8th, and 9th of July at the Mission of the Sacred Heart, among the Coeur-d'Alenes. Thence, I continued my route for St. Ignatius with Father Congiato, and completed the trip in a week; not, however, without many privations, which deserve a short mention here.

Imagine thick, untrodden forests, strewn with thousands of trees thrown down by age and storms in every direction; where the path is scarcely visible, and is obstructed by barricades, which the horses are constantly compelled to leap, and which always endanger the riders. Two fine rivers, or rather great torrents,—the Coeur-d'Alene and St. Francis Borgia,—traverse these forests in a most winding course; their beds are formed of enormous, detached masses of rock, and large slippery stones, rounded by the action of the water. The first of these torrents is crossed thirty-nine times, and the second thirty-two times, by the only path; the water often comes to the horse's belly, and sometimes above the saddle. It is considered good luck to escape with only the legs wet. The two rivers are separated by a high mountain, or rather a chain of mountains, called the Bitter Root chain. The sides of these mountains, covered with thick cedar forests, and an immense variety of firs and pines, present great difficulties to the traveller, on account of the great number of trees which lie broken and fallen across the path, and completely cover the soil. To these obstacles must be added immense fields of snow, which have to be crossed, and which are at times from eight to twelve feet deep. After eight hours' painful march, we arrived at a beautiful plain enamelled with flowers, which formed the summit of Mount Calvary, where a cross was raised on my first passage, sixteen years ago. In this beautiful situation, after so long and rude a course, I desired to encamp; but Father Congiato, persuaded that in two hours more we should reach the foot of the mountain, induced us to continue the march. When we had made the six miles which we supposed we had before us, and twelve miles more, darkness overtook us in the midst of difficulties. On the eastern side of the mountain we found other hills of snow to cross, other barricades of fallen trees to scramble over; sometimes we were on the edge of sheer precipices of rock, sometimes on a slope almost perpendicular. The least false step might precipitate us into the abyss. Without guide, without path, in the most profound darkness, separated one from the other, each calling for help without being able either to give or to obtain the least assistance, we fell again and again, we walked, feeling our way with our hands, or crawled on all fours, slipping or sliding down as best we could. At last a gleam of hope arose; the heard the hoarse murmur of water in the distance: it was the sound of the waterfalls of the great stream which we were seeking. Each one then directed his course towards that point. We all had the good fortune to arrive at the stream at last, but one after another, between twelve and one o'clock in the night, after a march of sixteen hours, fatigued and exhausted, our dresses torn to rags, and covered with scratches and bruises but without serious injuries. While eating our supper, each one amused his companions with the history of his mishaps. Good Father Congiato admitted that he had made a mistake in his calculation, and was the first to laugh heartily at his blunder. Our poor horses found nothing to eat all night in this miserable mountain gap.

I cannot omit here testifying my indebtedness to all the Fathers and Brothers of the Missions of the Sacred Heart and of St. Ignatius, for their truly fraternal charity towards me, and the efficacious aid which they rendered me towards fulfilling the special mission which had been intrusted to me.

As Father Congiato keeps the Very Reverend Father General informed of the actual state of the Missions of the mountains, it is unnecessary for me to enter into all its details; I recommend, especially, these poor children of the desert to his paternal attention and charity, and to our immediate Superiors in this country.

Divine Providence will not, I hope, abandon them. They have already a great number of intercessors in heaven, in the thousands of their children dead shortly after baptism, in the number of good Christian adults among them, who, having lead good lives, have quitted this world in the most pious dispositions, they can especially count upon the protection of Louise, of the tribe of Coeur-d'Alenes, and of Loyola, chief of the Kalispels, whose lives were an uninterrupted series of acts of heroic virtue, and who died almost in the odor of sanctity.

On the 22d of July I left the Mission of St. Ignatius, accompanied by Father Congiato with some guides and Indian hunters. The distance to Fort Benton is about two hundred miles. The country for the first four days is picturesque, and presents no obstacle to travelling. It is a succession of forests easily traversed, of beautiful prairies, impetuous torrents, pretty rivulets; here and there are lakes, from three to six miles in circumference, whose waters are clear as crystal, well stored with fish of various kinds: nothing can be more charming than the prospect. We called one of the largest of these lakes, St. Mary.

On the 26th of July we crossed the mountain which separates the sources of the Clarke River from those of the Missouri, at the 48th degree of north latitude and the 115th of longitude. The crossing does not take more than half an hour, and is very easy even for wagons and carts. At the eastern base of the Rocky Mountains the plains are mountainous, and almost destitute of timber; we crossed several small streams before we reached the Sun River, and followed down its valley almost to its mouth. We visited the great falls of the Missouri on our way: the principal fall is ninety-three feet high. Father Hoecken and Brother Magri met us in this vicinity. On the 29th we arrived at Fort Benton, a post of the St. Louis Fur Company, where we received the greatest attention from all its inmates; we feel particularly obliged to Mr. Dorson, the superintendent of the fort, for his continued kindness and charity to all our missionaries. May the Lord protect and reward him! The Blackfeet occupy an immense territory in this neighborhood; they reckon from ten to twelve thousand souls in the six tribes which compose this nation. They have been asking for Black Gowns (priests) for many years, and their desire appears universal. In my visit to them in 1846, they begged me to send a Father to instruct them.

Father Hoecken is now in these parts, and I have just read with the greatest pleasure, in the "Annals of the Propagation of the Faith," that the work of the conversion of the Blackfeet has been commenced, with the entire approbation of the Very Reverend Father General.

On our arrival in the neighborhood, we found a large number of Indians encamped around and near the fort. It was the period for the annual distribution of presents. They manifested their joy at the presence of a missionary to their country, and hoped that "all would open to him their ears and heart." The chief of a large camp, in one of our visits, related to us a remarkable circumstance, which I think worthy of mention.

When Father Point was among the Blackfeet, he presented some crosses to many chiefs as marks of distinction, and explained to them their signification, exhorting them, when in danger, to invoke the Son of God, whose image they bore, and to place all their confidence in him. The chief who related these details, was one of a band of thirty Indians who went to war against the Crows. The Crows having got upon their trail, gathered together in haste and in great multitudes to fight and destroy them. They soon came up with them in a position of the forest where they had made a barricade of fallen trees and branches, and surrounded them, shouting ferociously the dreaded war-cry. The Blackfeet, considering the superior numbers of the enemy who thus surprised them, were firmly persuaded that they should perish at their hands. One of them bore on his breast the sign of salvation. He remembered the words of the Black Gown (Father Point), and reminded his companions of them; all shouted, "It is our only chance of safety." They then invoked the Son of God, and rushed from the barricade. The bearer of the cross, holding it up in his hand, led the way, followed by all the rest. The Crows discharged a shower of arrows and bullets at them, but no one was seriously injured. They all happily escaped. On concluding his statement, the chief added with energy and feeling: "Yes, the prayer (religion) of the Son of God is the only good and powerful one; we all desire to become worthy of it, and to adopt it."

My intention, when I left General Harney, was, with his consent, to go all the way to St. Louis on horseback, in the hope of meeting a large number of Indian tribes, especially the large and powerful tribe of Comanches. I was obliged to renounce this project, for my six horses were entirely worn out, and unfit for making so long a journey; they were all more or less saddle-galled, and, not being shod, their hoofs were worn in crossing the rocky bottoms of the rivers, and the rough, rocky mountain roads.

In this difficulty, I ordered a little skiff to be made at Fort Benton; worthy Mr. Dawson, superintendent of the Fur Company, had the very great kindness to procure me three oarsmen and a pilot. On the 5th of August I bade adieu to Fathers Congiato and Hoecken, and dear Brother Magri, and embarked on the Missouri, which is celebrated for dangers of navigation—snags and rapids being numerous in the upper river.

We descended the stream about 2400 miles in our cockle-shell, making fifty, sixty, and sometimes, when the wind favored us, eighty miles a day. We took the first steamboat we met, at Omaha City. The steamer made about 700 miles in six days, and on the 23d of September, vigil of our Lady of Mercy, we entered the port of St. Louis.

During this long trip on the river we passed the nights in the open air, or under a little tent, often on sandbanks, to avoid the troublesome mosquitoes, or on the skirts of a plain, or in an untrodden thick forest. We often heard the howlings of the wolves; and the grunting of the grizzly bear, the king of animals in these parts, disturbed our sleep, but without alarming us. In the desert one perceives that God has implanted in the breast of the wild beasts the fear of man. In the desert, also, we are enabled in a particular way to admire and to thank that Divine Providence which watches with so much solicitude over his children. There is admirably verified the text of St. Matthew: "Consider the birds of the air, they sow not, but your Heavenly Father feeds them; are ye not of much more value than they." During the whole route, our wants were constantly supplied; yes, we lived in the midst of the great abundance. The rivers furnished us excellent fish, water-fowl, ducks, geese, and swans; the forests and plains gave us fruits and roots. We never wanted for game: we found everywhere either immense herds of buffaloes, or deer, antelope, mountain sheep or big-horns, pheasants, wild turkeys, and partridges.

On the way, along the Missouri, I met thousands of Indians of different tribes: Crows, Assiniboins, Minataries, Mandans, Rickaries, Sioux, &c. I always stopped a day or two with them. I received the greatest marks of respect and affection from these hitherto untutored children of the plains and mountains, and they listened to my words with the utmost attention. For many years these poor tribes have desired to have missionaries and to be instructed.

My greatest, I may say almost my only consolation, is to have been the instrument, in the hand of Divine Providence, of the eternal salvation of a great number of little children; of about nine hundred I baptized, many were sickly, and seemed only to wait for this happiness, to fly to God, to praise him for all eternity.

To God alone be all the glory; and to the Blessed Virgin Mary, our most humble and most profound thanks for the protection and benefits received during this long journey. After having travelled, by land and river over 8314 miles, and 6950 on sea, without any serious accident, I arrived safe and sound at St. Louis, among my dear brethren in Jesus Christ. I am with the most sincere respect,

Your servant in Christ,
P.J. DE SMET, S.J.

Interior of St. Mary's Church
Flat-head Mission, Communion at Easter

New Indian Sketches

LETTER OF FATHER DE SMET.

ST. LOUIS UNIVERSITY, DEC. 1, 1861.

DEAR SIR:

IN my letter of Nov. 10th, 1859, I alluded to the Skalzi Indians. Allow me to add fuller details concerning that tribe.

I visited these good savages, for the first time, in the summer of 1845, on which occasion I had the happiness to regenerate all their little children in the holy waters of baptism, as well as a large number of adults. I saw these dear children again in 1859; and the visit filled me with inexpressible joy, because they had remained faithful,—true to the faith, and fervent and zealous Christians. They were the consolation of their missionaries, and shone conspicuous by their virtues among the tribes of the Rocky Mountains. They were especially distinguished by an admirable simplicity, a great charity, and a rare honesty in all their dealings with their neighbors, and an innocence of manners worthy of the primitive Christians. A short account of this interesting tribe and the country which they inhabit, will doubtless please you.

The two tribes of the Kootenays and Flat-bows number over a thousand souls. They are principally divided into two camps, and are known in their country under the name of Skalzi. One of these camps, numbering about three hundred, inhabits sometimes the neighborhood of the great Flathead Lake, and sometimes the great Tobacco Plain, which is watered by the Koetenay River,—the distance is about seventy miles. The Tobacco Plain is a remarkable spot, situated between the forty-ninth and fiftieth degrees of north latitude, and is the only great plain possessed by this camp. It is about fifty or sixty miles long, by fifteen or twenty miles in width. It resembles a large basin, surrounded by lofty mountains, which form a vast and beautiful amphitheatre, and present a picturesque sight. The plain has all the appearance of the dry bed of a vast lake. Towards the south the valley is gravelly, undulating, and covered with little hillocks, and patches here and there are susceptible of cultivation; the northern portion, on the contrary, has a uniform surface, and a considerable extent of excellent arable land. Though the land is very elevated, and far towards the north, the temperature is remarkably mild, severe cold being a rare occurrence, and the snow is seldom deep; it falls frequently during the season, but disappears almost as it falls, absorbed, perhaps, by the rarefaction of the atmosphere at this elevation, or, perhaps, driven off by the southern breeze, which blows almost uninterruptedly in the valley, and drives the snow off as it falls. Horses and horned cattle find abundant pasture during the whole year. The large river, called indifferently the Koetenay, the McGilvray, and the Flat-bow River, flows through the entire valley. It rises to the northwest of this region, and its course is towards the southeast for a considerable distance. The waters of this great river are increased by a large number of brooks and beautiful rivulets, which have their source, for the most part, in the lovely lakes or numerous basins of these beautiful mountains. Many of these streams present to the eye the most charming scenes in their course. The noise of their waters and the sweet murmur of their falls are heard at some distance, and the eye is charmed by their descent from height after height, and their succession of cascades, from which they escape to the plain, covered with foam, and, as it were, exhausted by the struggles of the way. These mountain torrents will some day be the sites of mills of every description. Coal exists in many portions of the country, lead is found in abundance, and I venture to say that more precious minerals repose in the bosom of the mountains, and will one day be brought to light there.

The Indians have devoted themselves to agriculture for some years past. They cultivate little fields of maize, barley, oats, and potatoes, all of which ripen. It is rare that the frost injures the crops before the season of harvest. Their small fields cannot be extended, owing to the want of instruments of agriculture. They are compelled to turn the earth with instruments of the most primitive construction, such as Adam may have used in his day. The pointed stick made of a very hard wood, is what they have used from ages immemorial to dig up the *comach,* the bitter-root, the *wapatoo (sagitta folia,* the *caious*, or biscuit-root, and other vegetables of the same description. These Indians are very industrious. They are rarely unemployed. Their time is fully occupied in making bows and arrows, lines and hooks, or in hunting and fishing, or seeking roots or wild fruits for their numerous families. They extend their hunt often to the great plains of the Blackfeet and the Crows, to the east of the Rocky Mountains, on the upper waters of the Missouri and the Sascatshawin. Deprived as they are of agricultural instruments and fire-arms, they are always in want, and they may be said to keep a perpetual Lent.

The missionaries furnished them with a few ploughs and spades. Last year I forwarded to them, by the steamer of the Missouri Fur Company at St. Louis, some necessary agricultural implements, such as ploughs, &c.; but the boat was burned with all her cargo above the Yellowstone river.

It is much to be regretted that no more can be done for these good Indians, for, of all the mountain tribes, they are at once the best disposed and the most necessitous. The beau-ideal of the Indian character, uncontaminated by contact with the whites, is found among them. What is most pleasing to the stranger, is to see their simplicity, united with sweetness and innocence, keep step with the most perfect dignity and modesty of deportment. The gross vices which dishonor the red man on the frontiers, are utterly unknown among them. They are honest to scrupulosity. The Hudson Bay Company, during the forty years that it has been trading furs with them, has never been able to perceive that the smallest object had been stolen from them. The agent of the Company takes his furs down to Colvile every Spring, and does not return before Autumn. During his absence, the store is confided to the care of an Indian, who trades in the name of the Company, and on the return of the agent, renders him a most exact account of his trust. I repeat here what I stated in a preceding letter, that the store often remains without any one to watch it, the door unlocked and unbolted, and the goods are never stolen. The Indians go in and out, help themselves to what they want, and always scrupulously leave in place of whatever article they take its exact value.

The following anecdote will serve to give an idea of the delicacy of conscience of these good Indians.

An old chief, poor and blind, came from a great distance, guided by his son, to consult the priest; his only object being to receive baptism, if he should be considered worthy of the privilege. He stated to the missionary, that, in spite of his ardent desire to be baptized, he had not dared to approach the priest for that purpose, owing to a small debt of two beaver skins (say ten dollars) which he had contracted. "My poverty," said he, "has always prevented me from fulfilling this obligation; and until I had done so, I dared not gratify the dearest wish of my heart. At last I had a thought. I begged my friends to be charitable to me. I am now in possession of a fine buffalo robe: I wish to make myself worthy of baptism." The missionary, accompanied by the old man, went to the clerk of the Company to learn the particulars of the debt. The clerk examined the books, but said that no such debt existed. The chief still insisted on paying, but the clerk refused to take the robe. "Have pity on me," at last exclaimed the worthy old man, "this debt has rendered me wretched long enough; for years it has weighed on my conscience. I wish to belong to the blameless and pure prayer (religion), and to make myself worthy of the name of a child of God. This buffalo robe *covers* my debt," and he spread it on the ground at the feet of the clerk. He received baptism, and returned home contented and happy.

A young Kootenay who had been baptized in infancy, during my first visit in 1845, had emigrated with his parents to the Soushwaps in the mountainous regions near Fraser River. His parents desired to marry him to a young woman who was as yet unbaptized; he had a sister in the same condition. It was resolved that the three should make the long journey of many weeks' travel, to reach the Mission, in order that both sacraments might be received. On their arrival, their ardent faith, and praiseworthy earnestness, were the admiration of the whole village. The fervent missionary, Father Menetry, instructed these zealous neophytes, and prepared them for holy baptism. The young man, who had not seen a priest since 1845, had prepared himself to approach the tribunal of penance, for the first time, in order to make his first communion, and to receive the nuptial benediction with the proper dispositions. On the day appointed for the administration of all these sacraments, the young Kootenay presented himself with an humble and modest air at the confessional. He held in his hands some bundles of cedar chips, about the size of ordinary matches, and divided into small bunches of different sizes. After kneeling in the confessional and saying the confiteor, he handed the little bundles to the priest. "These, my father," said he, "are the result of my examination of conscience. This bundle is such a sin: count the chips and you will know how many times I have committed it;

the second bundle is such a sin,'' and so he continued his confession. His confession was accompanied with such sincere signs of grief, that his confessor was affected to tears. It is impossible not to be struck with admiration for the simplicity of heart which led our young savage, in his desire to perform this duty with the utmost exactitude, to this new method of making a confession; but still more admirable is the adorable grace of the Holy Ghost, who thus sheds His gifts upon these, His poor children of the desert, and, if I may dare to say so, adapts himself to their capacity.

In their zeal and fervor the Kootenays have built a little church of round logs on the great Tobacco Prairie. They carried the logs,—which averaged from twenty to twenty-five feet in length,—in their arms a distance of more than a quarter of a mile, and raised the walls of the new church, as it were, by main force. The exterior is covered with straw and sods. In this humble house of the Lord they meet morning and evening, to offer to the Great Spirit their fervent prayers,—the first-fruits of the day. How striking is the contrast between this little church of the desert and the magnificent temples of civilization, especially in Europe. The majesty of these churches, their fine pictures, the sculpture which adorns their walls, and their imposing proportions, inspire the beholder with admiration and awe: yet, on entering this little cabin, consecrated to the Great Spirit in the desert, erected by poor Indians,—on contemplating the profound recollection, the sincere piety depicted on their features,—on hearing them recite their prayers, which seem to rise from the bottom of their heart, it is difficult to refrain from tears, and the spectator exclaims: ''Indeed, this poor and humble church is the abode of the Lord and the house of prayer; its whole beauty lies in the piety, zeal, and fervor of those who enter there!''

In this humble church are now performed all the religious ceremonies of baptism and marriage. The Indians defer them until the appointed season for the arrival of the missionaries; they then come in from all parts of the country. "How beautiful are the feet of those who announce the Gospel of peace." The priest of this Mission finds the truth of the words, "*Jugum meum suave:* my yoke is sweet." No sooner has he arrived than all crowd round him, as beloved children to greet, after a long absence, a father whom they tenderly venerate. Even the hands of infants are placed in those of the missionary by their mothers. A long conference then follows. The priest gives and receives all news of important events which have happened since the last meeting, and regulates with the chiefs the exercises to be followed during his present visit. He gives two instructions a day to adults, and catechises the children; he helps them to examine well their consciences, and to make a good confession: he prepares them to approach worthily the Holy Table, instructs the catechumens and admits them to baptism, together with the children born during his absence; he renews and blesses all new marriages; and, like a father, settles any difficulties which may have arisen. Some he encourages and strengthens in the Faith, and removes the doubts and soothes the inquietudes of others. In a word, he encourages all these good neophytes to know the Lord, to serve Him faithfully, and love Him with all their hearts.

If the days of the missionary are thus filled with labor and fatigue, he has his full recompense of merit and consolation. He counts them among the happiest days of his life. The Reverend Father Menetry, their missionary, during his visit in 1858, baptized fifty children and thirty adults, blessed forty marriages, and heard over five hundred confessions.

The great chief of the Kootenays, named Michael, recalls in the midst of his tribe the life and virtues of the ancient patriarchs. His life is that of a good and tender father, surrounded by a numerous family of docile and affectionate children. His camp numbers four hundred souls. They are all baptized, and they walk in the footsteps of their worthy chief. It is truly a delightful spectacle to find in the bosom of these isolated mountains of the

Columbia river, a tribe of poor Indians living in the greatest purity of manners, and leading a life of evangelic simplicity. They are almost deprived of the succors of religion, and receive the visit of a priest but once or twice in the course of a year.

The sleep of a missionary among the Indians is always deep. His entire day, and a great part of the night, is spent in instructing them, and arranging the affairs of their conscience. When his work is done, his slumber is profound, and it is not surprising that he hears nothing that passes around him. I wish to add, at this point, a little chapter on the subject of Indian dogs. "*Experte crede Roberto.*"

Having had much experience in this matter myself, I give ready and implicit faith to the statement made to me by Father Menetry, as to the conduct of the dogs of the Kootenays. It is the reverse side of his beautiful description of life among this tribe. All is not beauty and pleasure in this charming wilderness. It is well that travellers at a distance should be forewarned of what they may expect, that they may provide themselves for the occasion. If the traveller has only one tent, he must be careful before he retires to barricade the entrance well, and surround it with brush; he must stop every crack and cranny, and carefully hang out of reach not only all his provisions, but any thing made of leather, or that has once had connection with flesh, otherwise, he will find on waking, that himself and his cattle are deprived of provender. The Indian dogs are as bad as their masters are good. Their masters abhor theft, but these dogs make it their business, and subsist entirely by pilfering. These dogs are found to the number of six or seven in each family: each member owns one or two; they live on bones and the crumbs which fall from the frugal table of their poor masters, and I can assure you that very little is left from the meal of an Indian, who considers it a duty to eat all that is set before him, and is by no means nice at table. The dogs, therefore, are left to provide for themselves as best they can. For the most part, they work by night, and become very cunning and expert: hunger sharpens their rapacious instincts. Father Menetry assures us, that he has very often awoke in the morning as poor as Job, every thing having been carried off during the night. It was in vain that he had taken every precaution which prudence suggested before going to bed, the industry of these nocturnal marauders got the better of all his care. Sleeping like a log after the fatigues of the day, he never heard the noise made by the thieves during their stay, though they often fought with one another in his tent over their spoils. The more vigilant savages were frequently aroused by the racket made in his tent, and were in the habit of coming to his rescue. Sometimes a good old Indian dame, armed with a big stick, would present herself suddenly upon the field of battle, dealing her blows right and left upon the combatants; again, a stalwart young savage would venture into the Father's tent to disperse these midnight marauders, and restore peace. Occasionally, the good Father himself would be aroused by the noise of the howling of the dogs and the cries of those who had come to protect him. They would then set to work to repair, though rather too late, the breaches made in his fortifications, stopping up every hole, and barricading the entry afresh. He would then lie down again, at the risk of another attack from these indefatigable robbers.

At last a council of chiefs was held on the subject, in which it was resolved to put an end to these scenes, so annoying to the missionary. They therefore surrounded his tent with an inclosure impenetrable to dogs. They went further, even, and set to work, in good earnest, to build a presbytery with two apartments, attached to the church. One room was made to serve for a sleeping-room, and the other to meet in, and for private conference with the priest. The good savages replaced, each time, the provisions and other objects stolen by their dogs. Taking the food as it were, from their own mouths and from those of their children, that the Father might not suffer from hunger; for fear that the want of necessaries might shorten his stay among them.

It appears from these little details, that Charity, the eldest daughter of Religion, flourishes in the soul of the simple savage, as well as in that of the children of Civilization. Though poorer and more humble among them, charity is not less industrious, not less beautiful: it is more simple and candid with them, and therefore more attractive.

P.J. DE SMET, S.J.

Indian Woman Flattening the Head of her Child

A VOCABULARY OF THE SKALZI,

OR KOETENAY TRIBE, INHABITING THE ROCKY MOUNTAINS ON THE HEADWATERS OF THE CLARKE AND MACGILVRAY RIVERS.

TAKEN DURING MY TRIP OF 1859.

Titto.	Father.
Kettitto.	My father.
Tittonis.	Thy father.
Tittowis.	His father.
Kittĕtōnelgle.	Our father.
Tittoniskelg.	Your father.
Galg.	Son.
Kannagalgli.	My son.
Galgtinis.	Thy son.
Galgliis.	His son.
Kannagenaggle.	Our son.
Galgniskilg.	Your son.
Kâkittĕgle.	My house.
Akitglênis.	Thy house.
Kakitglenêgle.	Our house.
Akitgleniskilg.	Your house.
Koos.	Pipe.
Kakoosh.	My pipe.
Koosnish.	Thy pipe.
Koosish.	His pipe.

Kakooshnêgle.	Our pipe.
Akitsēmmelg.	Knife.
Kakessemmelg.	My knife.
Akessemmelgnis.	Thy knife.
Akessemmelgis.	His knife.
Kakkesemmelgnegle.	Our knife.
Joukisitnemme	Day.
Kitsilgmouiêt.	Night.
Sookĕne.	Good.
Tsênnin.	Bad.
Pekkêk.	Long ago.
Makke.	Soon.
Tittekête.	Man.
Tittekêtĕnintik.	Men.
Pelgki.	Woman.
Pelgkïmintik.	Women.
Nitstêhelg.	Young man.
Nitstêhelgnintik.	Young men.
Nutkwinne.	One.
Ash.	Two.
Kelgsê.	Three.
Gâtse.	Four.
Yikko.	Five.
Nmissê.	Six.
Wistelggle.	Seven.
Ogwātsê.	Eight.
Kykittŏwĕ.	Nine.
Ittŏwĕ.	Ten.
Ittowonglenkkwe.	Eleven.

Ittowongleäsh.	Twelve.
Ittowinnŏwe.	One hundred.
Ittowolg ittowinnowo.	One thousand.
Yŏwo.	Twenty.
Kattesennĕwe.	Thirty.
Gatsennŏwo.	Forty.
Jikunnĕwo.	Fifty.
Nmissennewo.	Sixty.
Westenenne.	Girl.
Egkomne.	Infant.
Kamma.	Mother.
Kennukglakkanelg.	My husband.
Kattelgnammo.	My wife.
Kessŭwi.	My daughter.
Kukkètŏgammelg.	My brother.
Kolgglitskilg.	My sister.
Akkĕsĕmākkănik.	Indians.
Ekkĕglêm.	Head.
Ekkuktĕglê.	Hair.
Akkakkăne.	Face.
Akkīnnĕkelg.	Forehead.
Akukkowête.	Ear.
Akakkĕglelg.	Eye.
Ako.	Nose.
Akelgmanna.	Mouth.
Welgglonêk.	Tongue.
Akonannê.	Teeth.
Akokkegleggê.	Beard.
Akokêk.	Neck.

Akëglêke.	Arm.
Aki.	Hand.
Akitskyhi.	Fingers.
Akukkĕpĕ.	Nails.
Akulgglêk.	Body.
Akkuksâke.	Leg.
Akkĕglik.	Foot.
Akilskakkămak.	Toes.
Makke.	Bone.
Akitglêwi.	Heart.
Wennĕme.	Blood.
Kikkĕglēnām.	Village.
Nessōki.	Chief.
Kappilgglitit.	Warrior.
Kitsglêkilggla.	Friend.
Kîttęglāna.	House.
Yēlskīme.	Kettle.
Kakĕglem.	My head.
Kakëlglumma.	My throat.
Kákĕwettĕkêk.	My breast.
Kakenukkeglêke.	My stomach.
Kakĕwoom.	My belly.
Kakakkeglig.	My eyes.
Kaêkkoon.	My nose.
Kakelglumma.	My lips.
Kowwelgglōn̂êk.	My tongue.
Käkkĕglêk.	My backbone.
Kaäkkĕsāke.	My legs.
Kajouskennek.	My knee.

Kaäkkeglête.	My arm.
Kakĕgliek.	My foot.
Têwwo.	Gun, bow.
Akkĕ.	Arrow.
Akuttelg.	Axe.
Yakkĕsomelg.	Canoe.
Glenn.	Shoes.
Yakkyt.	Tobacco.
Ekkelglōmouët.	Sky.
Nettēnnīkkĕ.	Sun.
Kîtselgmittelgnukkăky.	Moon.
Akelgnōhōos.	Star.
Yokĕyitnēnnē.	Day.
Kilgmouit.	Night.
Nukkokĭgittĕnĕ.	Light.
Nêmmogonnê.	Darkness.
Woulgnêm.	Morning.
Glĕmāsït.	Spring.
Akkĕsōke.	Summer.
Suppĕnēkkoot.	Autumn.
Wennouït.	Winter.
Akkōmi.	Wind.
Numma.	Thunder.
Kelgglettelglig.	Lightning.
Akkeglukkekakkēk.	Rain.
Akkĕglo.	Snow.
Kappĕkamākê.	Hail.
Akinnĕkukko.	Fire.
Woö.	Water.

Akowīte.	Ice.
Ammāk.	Land.
Akkelggleït.	River.
Akukkōnōk.	Lake.
Akukglupgloït.	Valley.
Akŏwōgliït.	Mountain.
Akankammilg.	Island.
Nōki.	Stone.
Kămĭskăglaggănĕ.	Salt.
Nilgko.	Iron.
Kakammŏgōmoolg.	Hoe.
Akăniggelg.	Powder.
Akke.	Ball.
Akugglek.	Meat.
Kittekwakulggwa.	Flour.
Awomo.	Medicine.
Akenitsglaä.	Tree.
Akukglekkopilg.	Leaf.
Akitssĕkelg.	Bark.
Ṣahelg.	Grass.
Ġelgsi.	Dog.
Glukkŏpo.	Buffalo.
Nappĕko.	Black bear.
Kakki.	Wolf.
Suppĕky.	Deer.
Glôwwo.	Elk.
Sinna.	Beaver.
Akannukglam.	Snake.
Akkĕmakkê.	Egg.

Akkinnĕkāha.	Feathers.
Akowīte.	Wings.
Tiyakkegle.	Duck.
Egglêwĕ.	Pigeon.
Kiyakkeglo.	Fish.
Swakkămo.	Salmon.
Wiëlg.	Sturgeon.
Kakikkeglit.	My name.
Kammĕnukkĕglo.	White.
Kennehoos.	Red.
Kamkokukkōlg.	Black.
Kammakkēsin.	Yellow.
Kakkegloyittĕky.	Green.
Kowilgky.	Great.
Kitssekunnê.	Small.
Kissemakkĕkê.	Strong.
Tilgnemme.	Old.
Kitssekunnê.	Young.
Kissook.	Good.
Kĕsāhān.	Bad.
Kesahannelgkê.	Ugly.
Gettenukkēn.	Alive.
Kiëp.	Dead.
Kiskettegleït.	Cold.
Kuttemelggliït.	Warm.
Kammin.	I.
Ninko.	Thou.
Ninksish.	He.
Kammĕnelggle.	We.

Ninkŏmshkelg.	You.
Ninkoish.	They.
Tuno.	This.
Kappi.	All.
Yenakkenne.	Many.
Kelggle.	Who.
Akattêk.	Near.
Nōw sinnemomtĕke.	To-day.
Walgkŏwa.	Yesterday.
Kannewouit.	To-morrow.
Hê.	Yes.
Māts.	No.
Woussilg ikkĕne.	I eat.
Woussilg ikougle.	I drink.
Wousnenglukkapekanne.	I run.
Wounowesgoume.	I sing.
Woutskomnêne.	I sleep.
Woulsisgenni.	I speak.
Onuppegonne.	I see.
Outsglekelnē.	I love.
Onēpilne.	I kill.
Onesakkenoune.	I sit.
Onewekene.	I stand.
Woutsnagge.	I go.
Oulsinglewīno.	I am angry.
Oultakatinc.	I am lazy.
Oulsukkĕkokĭne.	I am glad.

11*

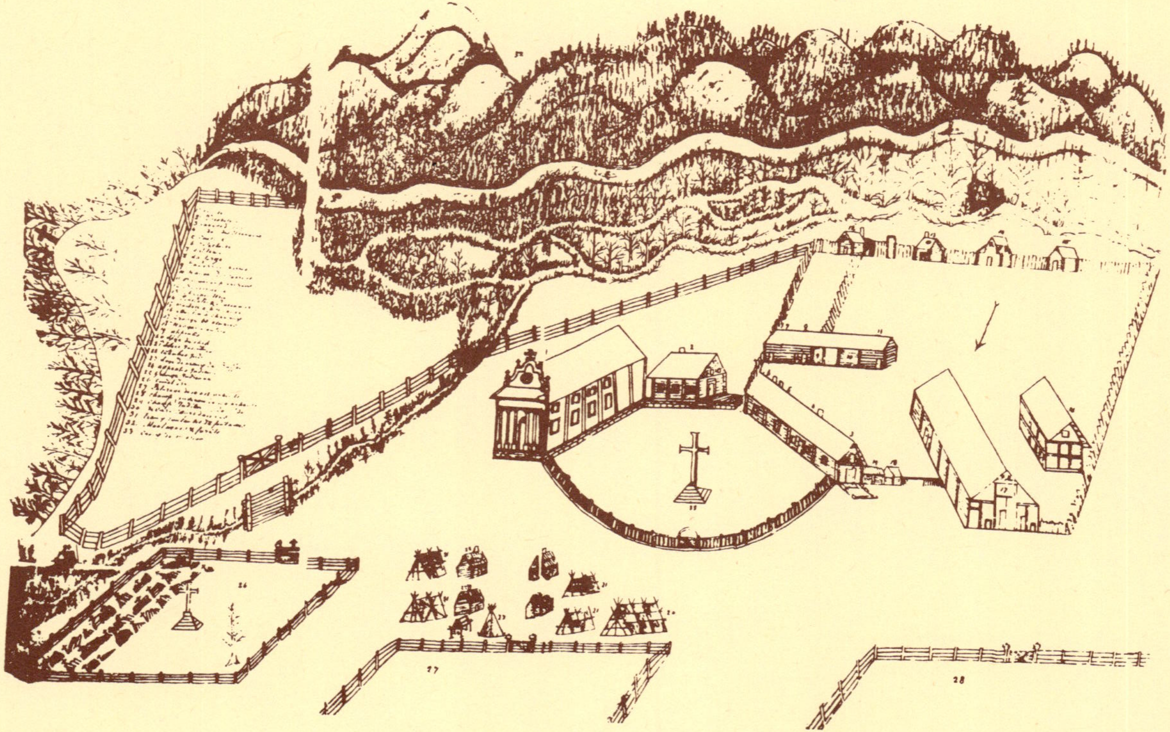

Sketch of Mission by Father Gilmore ca. 1860.

LETTER OF GENERAL HARNEY.

HEADQUARTERS, DEPARTMENT OF OREGON.
Fort Vancouver, W.T., June 1, 1859.

SIR:—I have the honor to report, for the information of the general-in-chief, the arrival at this place, on the 28th ultimo, of a deputation of Indian chiefs from the upper Pend-d'Oreilles, lower Pend-d'Oreilles, Flatheads, Spokans, Colville, and Coeur-d'Alene Indians, on a visit, sugggested by myself through the kind offices ofthe Reverend Father De Smet, who has been with these tribes the past winter, and has counselled them, both as an agent of the Government and in his clerical capacity, as to the advantages accruing to them by preserving peaceable and friendly relations with the whites at all times.

These chiefs have all declared to me the friendly desires which now animate them towards our people, and they assure me that their own several tribes are all anxiously awaiting their return, to confirm the peace and good-will they are hereafter determined to preserve and maintain. Two of these chiefs,—one of the upper Pend-d'Oreilles and the other of the Flatheads,—report that the proudest boast of their respective tribes, is the fact that no white man's blood has ever been shed by any one of either nation. This statement is substantiated by Father De Smet. The chiefs of the other tribes mentioned, state their people now regret they had been so deceived and deluded as to go to war with the whites the past year. They tender the most earnest assurances that such will never be the case again. All of these chiefs assert there will be no difficulty for the future as regards the whites travelling through their country, or in the occupation of it.

They request the Government to secure a reservation to their people, upon which they desire to live and be protected.

Kamiakin, the noted chief of the Yakimas, came in with these chiefs as far as Fort Walla-walla, with the intention of surrendering himself to my custody, but in consequence of an officious interference with these Indians on the part of Mr. T__________, agent for the Flatheads, Kamiakin became alarmed, and returned to his people. No censure is to be attached to Kamiakin for this act, and I have caused him to be notified that I am satisfied with his present peaceful intentions. . . . .

I have also the honor to inclose a copy of Father De Smet's report as to the Indian tribes he has visited the past winter, which shows that peace exists among themselves as well as with the whites; and from my own observation I am convinced that with proper care, another Indian war of any magnitude cannot soon occur in this department.

It gives me pleasure to commend to the general-in-chief the able and efficient services the Reverend Father De Smet has rendered.

I am, sir, very respectfully,
Your obedient servent,
W.S. HARNEY,
Brigadier-general commanding.

ASSISTANT ADJUTANT—GENERAL,
Headquarters of the Army, N.Y. City.

LETTER OF FATHER DE SMET.

FORT VANCOUVER, May 25, 1859.

DEAR CAPTAIN:

TOWARDS the end of last March, owing to the deep snows and the impracticableness of the mountain passes, I received your kind favor of the 1st of January of the present year. I am happy to learn that my request to the general, about bringing down to Vancouver a deputation of the various chiefs of the upper tribes, met with his approval. I have no doubt, from the happy dispositions in which I left them at Walla-walla, the general's advice and counsel will be cheerfully and punctually followed out by them, and will prove highly beneficial to their respective tribes, and consolidate the peace established last fall by Colonel Wright.

During my stay among the Rocky Mountain Indians, in the long and dreary winter, from the 21st of November last until the end of April, I have carried out, as far as lay in my power, the instructions of the general. I succeeded, I think, in removing many doubts and prejudices against the intentions of the Government, and against the whites generally, which were lurking in the minds of a great number of the most influential Indians. I held frequent conversations with the chieftains of the Coeur-d'Alenes, the Spokans, several of the Shuyelpees, or Kettlefalls, and the lower Kalispels, who had chiefly aided, particularly the two first-mentioned tribes, in their lawless and savage attacks on Colonel

Steptoe, and their war with Colonel Wright.

These various tribes, with the exception, perhaps of a small portion of lawless Kettlefalls, *and lower Kalispels,* are well disposed, and will faithfully adhere to the conditions prescribed by Colonel Wright, and to any future requests and proposals of treaties coming from Government. The upper Pend-d'Oreilles, the Kootenays, and Flatheads, I found, as years ago, strong friends and adherents to the whites, and I have every reason to think that they will remain faithful; they ever glory, and truly, that not a drop of a white man's blood has ever been spilled by any one of their respective tribes. When I proposed to them that from each tribe a chief should accompany me down to Fort Vancouver, to pay their respects to the general, and to listen to his advice, all eagerly consented, and they kept in readiness for the long journey as soon as the snow would have sufficiently disappeared. Meanwhile, Major Owen, agent among the Flatheads, arrived at St. Ignatius' Mission, and made known to me that he had received orders from the Superintendent of Indian Affairs and from Commissioner Mix, to bring down to Salem a chief of each tribe of the upper country. Upon this declaration I persuaded the Indians that as Major Owen had received orders from the highest authority he superseded me, and they should look upon him as their leader in this expedition, while I would follow on with them, as far as practicable and I would be allowed. The major having brought no provisions for them, I lodged the chiefs in my own tent, and provided them with all necessary supplies from the 16th of April until the 13th instant, the day on which we reached Walla-walla, and where the chiefs were liberally provided for by Captain Dent, in command of the fort. The deputation of chiefs was stopped at Walla-walla by Major Owen, to await an express he had sent on from Spokan prairie, with instructions to the superintendent at Salem. My own instructions from the general, according to your letter of the 1st of January, "To return to Fort Vancouver as early in the spring as practicable, for some contingency might arise requiring the general's presence elsewhere,'' hurried me down in compliance with said order. With regard to Kamiakin, and his brother Schloom, I held several talks with them in February, March, and April, and acquainted them with the general's order, wish, and desire in their regard, namely, that they should follow me, and surrender into his hands, assuring them, in the general's own words that ''the Government is always generous to a fallen foe, though it is at the same time determined to protect its citizens in every part of its territory,'' &c. They invariably listened with attention and respect. Kamiakin made an open avowal of all he had done in his wars against the Government of the country, particularly in the attack on Colonel Steptoe, and in the war with Colonel Wright. Kamiakin stated that he strongly advised his people to the contrary, but was at last drawn into the contest by the most opprobrious language the deceitful Telgawax upbraided him with in full council, in presence of the various chiefs of the Coeur-d'Alenes, Spokans, and Pelouses. Kamiakin repeatedly declared to me, and with the greatest apparent earnestness, that he never was a murderer; and, whenever he could, he restrained his people against all violent attacks on whites passing through the country. On my way down to Vancouver from St. Ignatius' Mission, I met him again, near Thompson's prairie, on Clarke's Fork. Kamiakin declared he would go down and follow me if he had a horse to ride, his own not being in a condition to undertake a long journey. I had none to lend at that moment. At my arrival in the Spokan prairie, meeting with Gerry, one of the Spokan chiefs, I acquainted him with the circumstance, and entreated him, for the sake of Kamiakin and his poor children, to send him a horse and an invitation to come on and to accompany the other chiefs to Walla-walla, and hence to Vancouver; it being his best opportunity to present himself before the general and superintendent, in order to expose his case to them and obtain rest and peace. Gerry complied with my request, and Kamiakin soon presented himself and joined the other chiefs. I had daily conversations with him until he reached Walla-walla: he places implicit confidence in the generosity of the general. I believe him sincere in his repeated declarations that henceforth nothing shall ever be able to withdraw him again from the path of peace, or, in his own words, "to unbury and raise the tomahawk against the whites." My candid impression is, should Kamiakin be allowed to return soon, pardoned and free, to his country, it will have the happiest and most salutary effect among the upper Indian tribes, and facilitate greatly all future transactions and views of Government in their regard. The Indians are anxiously awaiting the result, I pray that it may terminate favorably with Kamiakin. The sight of Kamiakin's children, the poverty and misery in which I found them plunged, drew abundant tears from my eyes. Kamiakin, the once powerful chieftain, who possessed thousands of horses and a large number of cattle, has lost all, and is now reduced to the most abject poverty. His brother Schloom, if he lives, will come in in the course of the summer. I left him at Clarke's Fork sickly and almost blind: he could only travel by small journeys. Telgawax, a Pelouse, I think is among the Buffalo Nez-Perces; from all I can learn, he has been the prime mover in all the late wars against Colonel Steptoe and Colonel Wright. His influence in not great, but he remains unceasing in his endeavors to create bitter feelings against the whites, whenever he can meet with an opportunity.

With the highest consideration of respect and esteem for our worthy general, and his assistant adjutant-general, I remain, dear Captain,

Your humble and obedient servent,

P.J. DE SMET, S.J.,

A. PLEASONTON,

Captain 2d Dragoons, A. Adjutant-general.

LETTER OF CAPTAIN PLEASONTON.

HEADQUARTERS, DEPARTMENT OF OREGON.
Fort Vancouver, W.T., June 1, 1859.

MY DEAR FATHER:

THE general commanding instructs me to inclose a copy of his special order, No. 59, of this date, authorizing you to return to St. Louis through the different tribes of the interior, which you are so desirous to visit once again, for the purpose of confirming them in their good disposition towards the whites, as well as to renew their zeal and intelligence in the elements of Christianity,—the means so signally productive of good-will and confidence, in your labors of the past winter, requiring such self-denial and resolution.

On your arrival in St. Louis, the general desires you to report by letter to the adjutant-general at Washington, when your relations with the military service will cease, unless otherwise ordered by the War Department.

The general is anxious that I should communicate to you the deep regret with which he feels your separation from the service, and in making the announcement he is assured the same feeling extends to all those who have in any way been associated with you.

By the campaign of last summer submission had been conquered, but the embittered feelings of the two races, excited by war, still existed, and it remained for you to supply that which was wanting to the sword. It was necessary to exercise the strong faith which the red man possessed in your purity and holiness of character, to enable the general to evince successfully towards them the kind intentions of the Government, and to restore confidence and repose to their minds. This has been done: the victory is yours, and the general will take great pleasure in recording your services at the War Department; for such services no one feels more sensibly than yourself the proper acknowledgment is linked with the hopes that are cherished in the fulfilment of a Christian duty.

Satisfied that all necessary blessings will be bestowed upon you, in whatever sphere of duty you may be called to serve, the general will always be happy to tender to you the evidences of his esteem and friendship. I remain, Father, with the highest respect,

Your most obedient servant,

A. PLEASONTON,

Captain 2d Dragoons, A. Adjt.-gen.

REV. P.J. DE SMET, S.J.,

Chaplain, &c., Fort Vancouver, W.T.

LETTER OF GENERAL HARNEY.

HEADQUARTERS, DEPARTMENT OF OREGON.
Fort Vancouver, W.T., June 3, 1859.

SIR:—I have the honor to inclose, for the information of the general-in-chief, an interesting report from the Rev. P.J. De Smet, describing the country of upper Washington Territory, in the vicinity of the Rocky Mountains, now occupied by various Indian tribes.

This report is valuable from the rare advantages Father De Smet possessed for many years, in his position as missionary among those tribes, to obtain accurate information of the country; and his purity of character will always give respect and importance to his statements.

The description he gives of the upper Clarke's Fork, the St. Mary's or Bitter Root valley, the valley of Hell's Gate Fork, the upper valleys on the headwaters of Beaver River, and the Kootenays country, in connection with his suggestion of collecting the remnants of the Indian tribes in Oregon and Washington Territories in that region upon a suitable reservation, is well worthy the serious consideration of the Government.

The country spoken of will not be occupied by the whites for at least twenty years: it is difficult of access, and does not offer the same inducements to the settler that are everywhere presented to him on the coast.

The system adopted in California of placing large numbers of

Indians upon a single reservation, and causing them to adopt summarily the habits of life of the whites, failed in consequence of the abrupt transition brought to bear upon these simple and suspicious people. The plan proposed by Father De Smet is not open to this objection: it places the Indians in a country abounding with game and fish, with sufficient arable land to encourage them in its gradual cultivation; and by the aid of the missionaries at present with them, that confidence and influence will be established over their minds, by degrees, as will induce them to submit to the restraints of civilization, when the inevitable decree of time causes it to pass over them.

From what I have observed of the Indian affairs of this department, the missionaries among them possess a power of the greatest consequence in their proper government, and on which cannot be acquired by any other influence. They control the Indian by training his superstitions and fears to revere the religion they possess, by associating the benefits they confer with the guardianship and protection of the Great Spirit of the whites. The history of the Indian race on this continent has shown that the missionary succeeded where the soldier and civilian have failed; it would be well for us to profit by the lessons its experience teaches, in an instance which offers so many advantages to the white as well as to the red man, and adopt the wise and humane suggestion of Father De Smet.

I am, sir, very respectfully,
Your most obedient servant,
W.S. HARNEY,
Brigadier-general commanding.

ASSISTANT ADJUTANT—GENERAL,
Headquarters of the Army, N.Y. City.

LETTER OF FATHER DE SMET.

FORT VANCOUVER, W.T., May 28, 1859.

DEAR CAPTAIN:

IN compliance with the request of our worthy brigadier-general, I herewith give you a short narrative of the upper Washington Territory, as yet occupied by various Indian tribes, as far as my views and observations may have extended during several years' residence in that region, and particularly during the last winter trip I performed under the special direction of the general.

The distance from Fort Walla-walla to the great Spokan prairie, through which the Spokane River flows, is about 150 miles. This whole region is undulating and hilly, and though generally of a light soil, it is covered with a rich and nutritious grass, forming grazing fields where thousands of cattle might be easily raised. It is almost destitute of timber until you are within thirty miles of the Spokan prairie, where you find open woods, and clusters of trees scattered far and wide; this portion, particularly, contains a great number of lakes and ponds, with ranges of long walls of large basaltic columns, and beds of basalt. The country abounds in nutritious roots (bitter-root, camash, &c.), on which principally the Indians subsist for a great portion of the year. The Spokan prairie is about thirty miles from north to south, and from east to west, bounded all around by well-wooded hills, and mountains of easy access. The soil is generally light, though covered with abundance of grass.

Along the base of the hills and the mountains patches of

several acres of rich arable land may be found. The Spokan prairie is claimed by the Coeur-d'Alene Indians. Taking Coeur-d'Alene Lake as a central point, their country may extend fifty miles to every point of the compass. The lake is a beautiful sheet of clear water, embedded amid lofty and high mountain bluffs, and shaded with a variety of pines, firs, and cedars; in its whole circumference to my knowledge, there is no arable land. The low bottoms in several of its many bays are subject to frequent and long inundations in the spring. The lake is about thirty miles in extent from south to north, its width throughout is from one to two or three miles. It receives its waters principally from two beautiful rivers, the St. Joseph and the Coeur d'Alene rivers, running parallel from east to west; each is from sixty to eight yards broad, with a depth of from twenty to thirty feet. After the spring freshet their currents are smooth and even, and are hardly perceptible for about thirty miles from their mouths, and until they penetrate into the high mountain region which separates their waters from those of Clarke's Fork and of the St. Mary's or Bitter Root River; their respective valleys are from one to three miles broad, and are much subject to inundations in the spring; the narrow strips of land which border the two rivers are of the richest mould. The deep snows in winter, the ice and water, keep these valleys literally blocked up during several months (last winter it continued for about five months). Small lakes, from one to three miles in circumstances, are numerous in the two valleys. Camash, and other nutritious roots and berries abound in them. Beautiful forests of pine, &c., are found all along. The mountains bordering the two valleys are generally of an oval shape, and well wooded; a few only are snow-topped during the greatest portion of the year. All the rivers and rivulets in the Coeur-d'Alene country abound wonderfully in mountain trout and other fish. The forests are well stocked with deer, with black and brown bears, and with a variety of fur-bearing animals. The long winters and deep snows must retard the settlement of this country.

Clarke's Fork, at its crossing below the great Kalispel Lake, is about forty miles distant from Spokan prairie. Clarke's Fork is one of the principal tributaries of the upper Columbia. From its entrance into the lake to the Niyoutzamin, or Vermilion River, a distance of about seventy miles, I counted thirty-eight rapids. You meet with a succession of rapids and falls to its very head. Before it joins the Columbia, for a distance of about thirty miles, its rapids and falls are insuperable. In its whole length Clarke's River has few spots of good and arable soil, with ranges of dense and thick forests. The upper portion of the river, and its upper tributaries, have a succession of large prairies of light soil filled with water-worn pebbles, indicating bottoms or beds of ancient lakes. All these prairies are covered with a luxuriant and nutritious grass, and owing, probably, to the position of the high mountains by which they are surrounded, they are little or not covered with snows in the winter season. Such are Thompson's prairie, Horse prairie, Camash prairie, Jaco prairie, Flathead Lake prairie, with several other minor grazing fields. Far and wide apart, spots of less or more acres of good arable land are found; but too few, indeed, to make it for years to come, a thickly settled portion for the whites. The country of the upper Clarke's Fork, the St. Mary's or Bitter Root valley, the valley of Hell's Gate Fork, the upper valleys on the Beaver headwaters, the Kootenay country within the 49th degree, and under the jurisdiction of the United States, appear to be laid out and designed by Providence, to serve as reserves for the remnants of the various scattered tribes of Oregon and Washington territory, at least for some years to come. This region, I should think, might contain all the Indians, and afford them the means of subsistence. The rivers could supply them with fish, the prairies with domestic cattle, deer and elk are still abundant, the buffalo grounds are not far off; wild edible roots and fruits are plenty; which in each section a sufficient portion of arable land might be found and reclaimed for their sustenance. Should all the remnants of Indians be gathered in this upper region, one single military post would suffice to protect them against all encroachments and infringements of evil-disposed whites on Indians, and of Indians on the rights of the whites. As the reserves are not laid out in Washington and Oregon Territories far and wide apart, surrounded and accessible on all sides by whites, experience teaches that it must lead to the speedy destruction of the poor Indianss. Liquor and its concomitants, sickness and vice, will soon accomplish the work. Providence has intrusted and placed these weak tribes under the care and protection of a powerful government, whose noble end has always been to protect and advance them. If aided and assisted, in a proper situation, with agricultural implements, with schools, mills, blacksmiths, &c., I have no doublt but thousands of the aborigines might be reclaimed, and live to bless their benefactors. In the topographical memoir of Colonel Wright's campaign, recently published (page 75), I read to this effect: "The government, in its wisdom and prudence, should make some timely provision for these many Indians by selecting for and placing them upon proper reservations, in order that they may not be caused to disappear by the fast-approaching waves of civilization and settlement, that must overtake and eventually destroy them." I have labored for several years among the upper tribes in the capacity of missionary. My companions have carried on the work to the present time, and will, I hope, continue their labors. The want of adequate means has greatly retarded one of the principal objects we had in view,—their civilization. We can all, and do, cheerfully testify to the good dispositions of these upper tribes. Should they be supplied with the necessary implements of agriculture, with oxen, &c., they would all work, and would soon place themselves above want and in comfortable circumstances. As for schools, all are anxious to have their children taught. These are a few points I desire to be allowed to present to the consideration of the general, if they can in anywise tend to the amelioration of the lot of Indians. With the highest sentiments of respect and esteem, I remain, Captain, Your humble and obedient servant,

P.J. DE SMET, S.J.,
Chaplain, &c., U.S.A.

A. PLEASONTON,
Captain 2d Dragoons, A. Adjutant-general.

BIBLIOGRAPHY

Bagley, C.B. *Early Catholic Missions in Old Oregon.* 2 vols., Seattle, WA. 1932.

Bischoff, William, S.J. *Jesuits in Old Oregon: A Sketch of Jesuit Activities in the Pacific Northwest, 1840-1940.* Caldwell, Ida. 1945.

Brown, William C. *The Indian Side of the Story.* Spokane, WA., 1961.

Burns, Robert I., S.J. *The Jesuits and the Indian Wars of the Northwest.* New Haven, Yale Press, 1966.

Chittenden, H.M. and A.T. Richardson. *Life, Letters and Travels of Father De Smet.* 4 vols. New York, 1905.

Corley, Patricia. *The Story of St. Mary's Mission.* Oakland, CA. 1941.

Davis, Rev. Wm. Lyle, S.J. *History of St. Ignatius Mission.* Spokane, WA. 1954

______."Journey of 1840". *Pacific Northwest Quarterly.* Vol. XXXV (1944), p. 126.

De Smet, Pierre-Jean, S.J. *Letters and Sketches, with a narrative of a Year's Residence Among the Indian Tribes of the Rocky Mountains.* Phila. 1843.

______. *New Indian Sketches.* New York, 1886.

______. *Origin, Progress and Prospects of the Catholic Mission to the Rocky Mountains.* Ye Galleon Press, Fairfield, WA. 1967.

______. *Oregon Missions and Travels Over the Rocky Mountains, 1845-46.* Ye Galleon Press ed. Fairfield, WA. 1978.

______. *Western Missions and Missionaries.* New York, 1859.

Dominica, Sister Mary, S.N.D. *Willamette Interlude.* Palo Alto, CA. 1959.

Drury, Clifford M. *Nine Years with the Spokane Indians: Diary, 1838-1848 of Elkanah Walker.* Glendale, CA. 1976.

______. *First White Women Over the Rockies.* 3 vols., Glendale, CA. 1963.

Edwards, Jonathan. *History of Spokane County.* W.H. Lever Pub. 1900.

Evans, Lucylle H. *St. Mary's in the Rocky Mountains.* Stevensville, Mont. 1976.

______. *Good Samaritan of the Northwest, A. Ravalli, S.J.* Stevensville, Mont. 1981.

Fahey, John. *The Flathead Indians.* University of Oklahoma, Norman, Okla., 1974.

Garraghan, Gilbert J., S.J. *The Jesuits of the Middle United States.* 3 vols. New York, 1938.

Hafen, Leroy R. (ed.) *The Mountain Men and the Fur Trade of the Far West.* Glendale, CA. 1964-72.

Hudson's Bay Record Society. "McLoughlin's Fort Vancouver Letters, 1844-46." Vol. VII, London, 1944, (E.E. Rich, ed.)

_______. "McLoughlin's Fort Vancouver Letters, 1839-44." Vol. VI, London, 1943, (E.E. Rich, ed.)

Johnson, Olga Weydemeyer. *Flathead and Kootenay.* Glendale, CA., 1969.

Kowrach, Edw. J., ed. N. *Blanchet's Historical Sketches of the Catholic Church In Oregon.* Ye Galleon Press, Fairfield, WA. 1983.

Kurz, Rudolph Friederich. *The Journal of Rudolph F. Kurz.* Ye Galleon Press, Fairfield, WA. 1964.

Landerholm, Carl. *Notices and Voyages of the Famed Quebec Mission to the Pacific Northwest.* Portland, Ore. 1956.

Laveille, E., S.J. *The Life of Father De Smet, S.J.* (English translation by Marian Lindsay) New York, 1915.

Lyons, Sister Letitia Mary, S.H.N. *Francis Norbert Blanchet.* Washington, D.C., 1940.

McKay, Harvey J. *St. Paul, Oregon, 1830-1890.* Portland, Ore., 1980.

Margaret, Helene. *Father De Smet.* New York, 1940.

Mengarini, Gregory S.J. (ed. Gloria Ricci Lothrop). *Recollections of the Flathead Mission.* Glendale, CA., 1977.

Muench, David and Donald G. Pike. *Rendezvous Country.* American West Pub. Co. 1975.

Palladino, L.B., S.J. *Indian and White in the Northwest.* Lancaster, PA. 1922.

Point, Nicolas, S.J. *Wilderness Kingdom: Life in the Rockies: 1840-1847.* (ed. J.P. Donnelly) New York, 1967.

Rich, E.E. *The Letters of Dr. John McLoughlin.* Vol. VI and VII, Hudson's Bay Record Society, 1943, 1944.

Ruby, Robert H. and John A. Brown. *The Spokane Indians.*Norman, Okla., 1970.

Schoenberg, Wilfred P., S.J. *Jesuits in Montana.* Portland, Ore. 1960.

_______. *Paths to the Northwest.* Loyola Press, Chicago, Ill., 1982.

Shea, John Gilmary. *History of the Catholic Missions Among the Indian Tribes of the United States, 1529-1854,* New York, 1854.

Teit, James A. *The Salishan Tribes of the Western Plateaus.* (ed. Franz Boaz) Washington, D.C., 1927-28.

Terrell, John Upton. *Black Robe.* New York, 1964

Thwaites, Reuben Gold. *Early Western Travels,* "De Smet's Letters and Sketches." Vol. XXVII, Cleveland, Ohio, 1906.

Turney-High, Henry Holbert. *The Flathead Indians of Montana.* Menosha, Wis., Memoir 48, American Anth. Asso. 1941.

Weibel, George, S.J. (Historicus), *"Fifty Years of Peaceful Conquest".* Gonzaga University Magazine, Vol. V, 1913-1914).

APPENDIX A

In regard to the spelling of Fort Colvile the following should be noted: The Hudson's Bay Company Post was named in honor of Andrew Colvile, Governor of the Company in London. The spelling of his name "Colvile" was used for the Company post. The later established fort of the United States Army at Pickney City, near present Colville, Washington and the present-day usage is "Colville."

APPENDIX B

Father De Smet was deeply impressed by the sincere Christian life of Louise Sighouin (Siuwheem) of the Coeur d'Alenes. He wrote in the first part of *New Indian Sketches*, a sympathetic study of her life. He himself had baptized her in 1842. She was such an outstanding woman of virtue that even to the present day she is still a legend and a vivid, living memory among the Coeur d'Alene Indians.

This Indian woman, the daughter of a Chief, a mother and a wife living in the mountain vastness of the Bitterroot Mountains led an exemplary, heroic life without the benefits of civilization. She was surrounded by native, blind depravity, and unrestrained, inter-tribal warring. "She was an oasis amid a sterile waste." Her personal deep-rooted faith led her to share the consolations of religion with others by instructing the young, especially the girls, by loving care for the sick and dying and by an ardent zeal for the conversion of her fellow-tribesmen.

Louise Sighouin's saintly life was marked by gentleness, patience, courage and cheerful confidence in God in the face of severe opposition by the tribal medicine-men. Father De Smet calls her "a valiant woman of the wilderness." Her husband told the missionary priest of the Mission; "she was full of the wisdom and spirit of God."

INDEX

G

H

I

COLOPHON

The Pierre-Jean De Smet NEW INDIAN SKETCHES *was printed in the workshop of Glen Adams, which is located in the sleepy country village of Fairfield, southern Spokane County, Washington state and one township removed from the Idaho line. The text was set in fourteen point Bembo type with running heads in eighteen point Mahogany. The title page was set in Baskerville Bold with the three words 'New Indian Sketches' in twenty-four point Castellar hand type from Yendall & Company, Risca, Monmouthshire, England. The text was set by Sharyn Brown using a model 7300 Editwriter computer photosetter. Camera darkroom work was by Millie Ferger using a model 660C DS twenty-four inch camera. Indexing was by Edward J. Kowrach. The initials used for opening chapters were taken from an old type book. The film was stripped by Dale La Tendresse with printing plates made by Tami K. VanWyk. The sheets were printed by Robert La Tendresse using a 28 inch model KORS Heidelberg press. Folding was by Garry Adams using a 22x28 three stage Baum folding machine. Assembly work was by the Ye Galleon crew. The paper stock is seventy pound Ivory Brokaw vellum. Binding was by Willem Bosch of Oakesdale, Washington, assisted by Gerrit Bosch and Bill Harnois. The books were sewn by Dorothy Dineen using a National book sewing machine. Gold foil stamping of the cases was by Willem Bosch Jr. This was a fun project. We had no special difficulty with the work.*

Athabasca River
JASPER HOUSE
COMMITTEES PUNCH BOWL
Athabasca Pass
Saskatchevan
ROCKY
North
127°
125°
123°
121°
119°
117°
115°
Tonquin Massacre took place about here
FORT HOPE
FORT LANGLEY
Strait of Juan de Fuca
BOW F
CALG
CONTINENTAL
B
FORT MC
FORT OKANAGAN
FORT COLVILLE
FORT NISQUALLY
COWLITZ
COLUMBIA
FORT CLATSOP
ASTORIA
FORT WILLIAM
FORT VANCOUVER
FORT SIMCOE
J. S. Smith here Winter 1828-1829
CAYUSES
SACRED HEART
SPOKANE HOUSE
COEUR D'ALENES
ST. IGNATIUS
DIVIDE
FLATHEAD
RIVER
FORT WALLA WALLA
WALLA WALLAS
ST. PAUL
THE OREGON TRAIL
Clearwater
ST. MARY
FORT OWEN
NEZ PERCES
UMPQUAS
Umpqua Massacre July 1828
Crooks stopped here Dec. 1811 and turned back
Hunt stopped here Dec 1811 and turned back
Vanderburgh killed here
FORT BOISE
Malheur
Overland Astorians East
Crooks
Hunt
Caldron Linn
Smith met Jackson & Sublette about here Aug 5 1829
TETON PASS
FORT HALL
Klamath Lakes
Mt. Shasta
Pitt
SHOSHONES
ROOT DIGGERS
BANNOCKS
Soda Springs
CACHE VALLEY
THE CALIFORNIA TRAIL OF LATER YEARS
Walker 1833
GREAT SALT LAKE
OGDENS HOLE
(Salt Lake City)
J. S. Smith spent Winter of 1827-1828 about here
American
Carson Lake
Walker Lake
PAIUTES
J. S. Smith, May and June, 1827
Stanislaus
ASHLEY'S
Utah Lake